LARGE PRINT

Gingold
Dog World
35011

DATE DUE

JUL 13, 2018	

PRINTED IN U.S.A.

dog
world

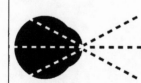This Large Print Book carries the
Seal of Approval of N.A.V.H.

dog
world

and the humans who live there

alfred gingold

Thorndike Press • Waterville, Maine

Published in 2005 by arrangement with Broadway Books,
a division of the Doubleday Broadway Publishing Group,
a division of Random House Inc.

Thorndike Press® Large Print Nonfiction.

The tree indicium is a trademark of Thorndike Press.

The text of this Large Print edition is unabridged.
Other aspects of the book may vary from the original edition.

Set in 16 pt. Plantin by Ramona Watson.

Printed in the United States on permanent paper.

Library of Congress Cataloging-in-Publication Data

Gingold, Alfred.
    Dog world : and the humans who live there / by Alfred
Gingold. — Large print ed.
        p. cm.
    ISBN 0-7862-7549-9 (lg. print : hc : alk. paper)
    1. Dogs.   2. Human-animal relationships.   3. Large type
books.   I. Title.
SF426.2G546 2005b
    636.7—dc22   2005001128

For Helen and Toby

As the Founder/CEO of NAVH, the only national health agency solely devoted to those who, although not totally blind, have an eye disease which could lead to serious visual impairment, I am pleased to recognize Thorndike Press★ as one of the leading publishers in the large print field.

Founded in 1954 in San Francisco to prepare large print textbooks for partially seeing children, NAVH became the pioneer and standard setting agency in the preparation of large type.

Today, those publishers who meet our standards carry the prestigious "Seal of Approval" indicating high quality large print. We are delighted that Thorndike Press is one of the publishers whose titles meet these standards. We are also pleased to recognize the significant contribution Thorndike Press is making in this important and growing field.

Lorraine H. Marchi, L.H.D.
Founder/CEO
NAVH

★ Thorndike Press encompasses the following imprints: Thorndike, Wheeler, Walker and Large Print Press.

contents

"I'd rather love a dog," said Coker. "He loves you back again. I saw such a nice pup yesterday. Think of all that love for ten and six — that's what they asked. And beat him all you like, he still thinks the world of you. It's nature."

— Joyce Cary, *The Horse's Mouth*

1. entering the dog world

COMMENCEMENT

*I loathe people who keep dogs.
They are cowards who haven't got
the guts to bite people themselves.*

— August Strindberg

I was not a dog person of any kind in the autumn of 2001, when my wife and I went for drinks at a down-at-the-heels but newly cool Brooklyn bar called O'Connor's. *Time Out New York* had recently cited the place as having the best moose head in the city, a designation that said more about the sorry state of the outer-borough moose head situation than the dubious magnificence of O'Connor's threadbare Bullwinkle. The thing presided over a joint where black-clad, ear-cuffed groovies drank alongside pregentrification habitués. On this night, there were no hipsters in evidence, only a ragged row of regulars slumped on stools in the dim light, staring into their drinks. No camaraderie, no Jell-O shots, no bar food, no pickup action, not even a television: a perfect Dark Bar, just the place for the serious talk we'd gone there to have.

Except for the dogs. What were the damn dogs doing in a bar?

They weren't creating a fuss; the three of them lay on the worn linoleum, taciturn as their masters. I admit I didn't like it. This is Brooklyn, not France, where dogs are permitted in restaurants and intensive care units. Dogs had just never been one of my things, though getting one was exactly what we were there to discuss.

The reason was our son, approaching thirteen and showing all the signs of impending adolescence. I say this knowing that we have been spared the full teen catastrophe. He sported no Mohawk, no piercings or tattoos. He never wafted around the house smelling all herblike. As of this writing, he still doesn't. Believe me, I know how lucky we are.

But there's no denying that our son, like many twelve-year-old boys, found us lacking — in wisdom, in charm, in spirit, in just about anything any reasonable person might expect from parents. I'm not complaining, merely pointing out the psychic challenge our little family faced.

As an only child, our son is all too often the center of both attention and tension. It's an old story, but I hated being an actor in it anyway. Sometimes I'd look at him and his brow would be furrowed with an intensity of worry that stopped me in my tracks. What was bothering him, I wondered, and what could I do about it?

The answer to the first question was everything, of course, and the answer to the second was nothing. And boy, did we share his pain, or at least remember the feeling. My wife and I vowed to help. Pets, we knew, are a time-honored way of providing kids with ready-made love and commitment, soul mates and companions through the uncertainties and agonies of adolescence.

This assumption is one I took on faith, having little experience to go by. My wife shared her early years with assorted fauna, including a cat, a hamster, and Jimmy the Mouse, of whom she still speaks fondly. I grew up in a pet-free home, aside from a goldfish that died within a week and a little alligator we brought home from Miami

Beach and soon flushed down the toilet, from whence it and its fellows would inspire generations of urban myths and Thomas Pynchon.

Pets, in the childhood view I carried unsullied into adulthood, were demanding, unpredictable, and unhygienic. This impression was not changed by the succession of half-dollar-size turtles we got for our son. The turtles inexorably grew big as dinner plates, requiring frequent and ever more repulsive tank cleanings. But at least the turtles didn't have to be walked. What could a dog do for our boy that the turtles didn't? I asked. My wife fixed me with a look that suggested she didn't believe my question was entirely sincere. "You can only relate to a turtle so far," she said.

Obviously, helping our son was a good reason to get a dog, but not compared to all the good reasons *not* to: the walks, the shedding, the poo, for starters. Before I could make my case, though, my wife was distracted by one of the bar dogs, a big brown mutt who'd gotten up to stretch and wandered over to our booth. My wife cooed, "Aren't you pretty?" and petted the creature. Pretty? I smiled gamely in the dog's general direction. Speaking of game, I noticed the dog had a faint odor. This

12

was before I learned that all dogs have a faint odor. (Actually, you're lucky if it's faint. The strange thing is that after a while you get to like it.) My wife petted the dog and the dog leaned into her hand. I noticed a little raw area on the dog's side, almost on her belly. The owner said quietly, "She's got a hot spot. Lying on the floor keeps it cool."

"A hot spot?" I said, apparently a shade too inquisitively, because the man dismounted from his stool and sat down with us. A hot spot, he explained, is an area that a dog rubs and licks until there is an actual break in the skin. Not surprisingly, it is generally considered a sign of stress. "I work at a dot com and I usually bring her in to work with me so that she doesn't have to be home alone all day," the man said. "We've had to lay off a lot of people lately and it's become a pretty sad place. That's when she started this compulsive grooming. They blame themselves, you know. They blame themselves."

Our chat continued. He told us about several of his past dogs and how, though all had been wonderful, none matched this one's sheer compassion for *la condition humaine;* all right, he didn't actually say anything in French, but he did make the dog sound like Gandhi incarnate. My wife asked questions solicitously. I nodded sympathetically, but the words of Victor Spinetti as the harried exec in *A Hard Day's Night* thrummed in my mind: "I could've done wonders in vivisection."

Eventually, man and beast went off dolefully into the night and my wife and I resumed our discussion. I was convinced I could never take proper care of a dog, the way that guy did. That guy was obviously a committed dog owner, tender and devoted. Also crazy as a loon. Therefore, I reasoned keenly, only crazy people should have dogs. Not that I claim to be playing with a full bag of clubs myself, only that my particular pathology does not lead me to seek solace with the four-legged. Even though we were still technically discussing the issue, in my heart I believed that the whole dog issue was closed.

You would think experience would teach me not to make rash predictions. But if experience has taught me anything, it is that experience rarely teaches me anything.

So it was that on a spring evening six months later, I was part of a small group milling excitedly around in the dingy basement of a local Catholic school. The instructor checked her watch and nodded to an assistant, who hit the PLAY button on a boom box, uncorking a tinny recording of "Pomp and Circumstance." My son held the leash firmly as certificates were handed out and flashes flashed. It was graduation day at obedience school. I chuckled, I beamed, and, as usual on such occasions, I regretted not having brought my camera.

The peculiar thing about this event was that I was prouder of the dog than of my son. I really shouldn't have been. My son had changed in many ways, all of them good: He'd become more patient and persistent and responsible. He regularly took the dog for his predinner pee walk and sometimes even the morning outing, which usually involves more serious business. He worked on training George every day and assumed the role of family dog whisperer, interpreting the creature's every twitch and snuffle with authority. These important steps on the path to adulthood were exactly what we'd hoped for.

The dog, on the other hand, hadn't changed much at all over the seven-week course that I wouldn't have signed up for at all if we'd managed to make any progress with any of the zillion (well, three) training manuals we tried. Sometimes he sat, sometimes he stayed, and sometimes he came.

Sometimes these actions were connected to our commands; more often they were connected to the greasy nubbins of Hebrew National franks and Muenster cheese that I diced before each class. Most often, though, he did what he did for reasons that may be explicable to a terrier, but not to you or me.

The truth is, George was not graduating cum laude. Whether too independent or too dim to do what was asked, George barely managed a gentleman's C, and he was the oldest dog in the class, too. At a year and half or so, his age in dog years meant he should have been in graduate school, if not out in the workforce, instead of here in the basement, tugging on the leash and snapping at the nasty bichon frise. His failure to perform did not endear him to the trainer, who preferred to lavish her attentions on dogs who would produce quicker results, like the Entlebucher pup whose first-rate sitting and staying skills reinforced my loathing of all things Swiss, especially their rotten dogs. At the time, it annoyed me deeply that George was the only dog in the class she never once used to demonstrate a task. This was before I knew that when trainers want to show how easy it is to bend a dog to your will,

16

they *never* demonstrate on a terrier.

Whichever family member worked with George would finish the session with stinky pockets and frayed nerves. Then we'd all stroll home, bickering meanly. I would have quit had I not felt obligated to set a good example for my son after the third class, when my wife refused ever to go again.

So why was I welling with pride over a creature who'd done little more than tolerate his classes, classes that constituted some of the worst evenings of my life?

My inner dog person was stirring.

Don't get me wrong. I don't send dog greeting cards or hang dog calendars on the wall. There are really very few breed-specific tchotchkes in my home. Within the first few months, I'd bought a mug, a fridge magnet, a rubber stamp, an all-Norfolk calendar, and a nice brooch for my wife, whom I knew did protest too much when she told me to quit it with the doggie doodads. I don't believe that George's attachment to our family is really "unconditional love," one of the great clichés of the Dog World.

The other, of course, is that a dog is man's best friend, and I don't buy that one either, especially since learning that its first expression was in a closing argument by a

17

Missouri lawyer named George Graham Vest. In 1869, Vest represented the owner of Old Drum, a hunting dog that made the mistake of wandering onto the property of a sheep farmer who was completely within his rights, if not a very nice person, in shooting the animal. Lawyer Vest laid it on with a trowel ("there, by his graveside will the noble dog be found . . ."), and his euphonious oratory carried the day, despite the fact that he did not have a legal leg to stand on.

I certainly don't consider George my best friend. That would be ridiculous. I do consider him my best-looking and most constant friend, though, and the only one who truly doesn't mind my tendency to repeat myself. I try to treat him with the respect he deserves. I almost never talk baby talk to him, at least not when we're out for walka-walkies (at home, different story). I do not, *not,* stand over him chanting "Do the cute thing!" when he does one of his innumerable cute things, as some in my family are wont to do. When a fellow dog walker praised George's angulation, I had no idea what he meant. I do now, though, sort of. I know the differences between dappled, brindled, and marled coats, but not if I have to explain them in, you know, words. As of this writing, I belong to no kennel clubs and subscribe to only one dog magazine, the *Whole Dog Journal*, a somber periodical with articles like "Reflections on Heartworm" and "Living with a Difficult Dog." I am, in short, not obsessed with the dog.

"Preoccupied" is more the word. Maybe tending toward "very preoccupied."

It helps that George is the cutest being I've ever seen, regardless of species. He is small, muscular, and peppy, and he has rough, tweedy fur — maybe it's hair, I always forget — of the precise rusty shade I have long dreamed of in a sport coat. He has a way of tilting his head when I say his name softly that I find ineffably endearing. But cuteness isn't everything. The world is full of cuteness that does little or nothing for me: pandas; ducklings; Meg Ryan.

George would probably have wormed his way into my heart, mind, and routine even if he weren't so damn cute, even now in the latish midrange of what has been a contentedly dogless, and mostly petless, life. The most casual survey of dog people and their significant others reveals that beauty isn't everything when dogs are concerned. Sometimes, it's absolutely nothing.

I fuss over George when he's sick and I fuss over him when he's well. I send him to a playgroup several days a week to give him intraspecies quality time. I will discuss the state of his bowels with anyone who cares to engage me on the subject. Just when my days of browsing endless rows of overpriced kids' toys are over, I am browsing endless rows of overpriced doggie toys. And often I buy them, particularly if they have a good squeak.

Like many neophyte dog owners, I've gone a little nutty. For example, one of my great pleasures in life has always been people watching. I've spent innumerable hours walking happily around the city, scoping the passing parade. Now when I walk down the street, my gaze rarely rises above knee level. I'm looking at dogs, not people. Who knew there were so many around? Familiarity has not bred contempt. It's bred affection, indulgence, and boundless curiosity.

For example, I wonder how George feels when we board him. He stays at a very nice kennel with a big outdoor area where the dogs can frolic, but I always spend the first few hours of separation feeling guilty and remorseful. I think of my friend's bulldog, Winston, who was kenneled for six months because of some job-related traveling my friend had to do. Ever since, if Winston sees my friend touch a piece of luggage, he climbs into it. George shows no such separation anxiety. He is plainly happy and relaxed when he goes off to the kennel and seems pretty much the same when he returns. I don't really know for sure that he's happy; I suppose he could be seething with resentment. It's the sort of thing I think about when I should be doing other things.

George has not only opened the door to new experiences, he has led to greater self-knowledge. I can honestly say that I know things about myself that I never knew pre-George. The most important thing I've learned is how much time I waste. I have always had a tendency to get lost in thought, to woolgather. Then I come to my senses and wonder where the time went. Now, however distracted I may be, I always know exactly where the time went, because I always know what I am thinking about: the dog. And what I am thinking about is what the dog is thinking about. That is, I am always thinking about what the dog *might* be thinking about. You can't ever really know such a thing, but who can resist wondering?

At any given moment, similar wonderment is blooming in the minds of many of the 44 million Americans who care for the nation's 65 million owned dogs. We are the human residents of the Dog World. We think about dogs by any means necessary.

This book is the story of my journey into dog personhood. I would like to say it is a journey that has left me older but kinder, wiser and with enhanced respect for all living creatures in the great chain of being. It's certainly left me older and, if not wiser, at least more knowledgeable about this new society of which I've become a part.

The most surprising discovery I've made en route is that there is a difference between a dog person and a person with a dog. Dog people are dog people forever, and if they don't have a dog at the moment, they probably will in the not-too-distant future.

On the other hand, dog ownership doesn't guarantee dog personhood. An elderly cocker spaniel in my neighborhood is walked daily by various members of a family. In the morning, it's usually Dad, leash in one hand, carefully folded *Times* in the other, a feat of multitasking that astounds me. In the evening, it's usually

Mom or Sis and their cell phones. I've never seen any of the walkers concentrating on the dog, or even looking at it much. The dog, fortunately, is low energy, and seems content to amble along, a-sniffing and a-peeing. There is no cruelty here. The dog is clearly well fed and cared for. But none of the individuals walking him is involved with him. They have a dog, but they're not dog people.

I'm not criticizing. I don't believe the world would necessarily be a better place if everybody in it were a dog person. There are Dog World qualities that creep me out — the funny voices we use to talk to our dogs, alternately sugary and booming, then use on people, too. There's the widely held assumption that all dog people share the same threshold of disgustingness. Many think nothing of gesticulating wildly with a hand that is holding a plastic bag of dogshit. I still have inhibitions about that sort of thing. I keep that arm close to my body, unobtrusively twisting my wrist in a way that doesn't feel so great, but enables me to keep the bag close in without actually, you know, bumping into my leg. The position is a little hard to maintain, so I try to keep street chats short when I'm holding.

What really defines a dog person is persistence of focus. Conversation, books, music — in the dog person's mind, all synaptic roads lead to the same place. Not exclusively and not so that we start talking to strange dogs on the street, although that's certainly been known to happen. But in a fundamental way, we experience the world through the prism of dog awareness.

And that's a good thing, for the most part. I have a raft of acquaintances whose names I don't know, but whose dogs' names I do. I watch agility trials on television, mostly identical border collies who look as if they've been drinking black coffee, and I *cheer*. With impunity and even aplomb, I incorporate into my daily conversation terms like alpha male, lead rather than leash, hot spot, gay tail, and Dudley Nose, a name I intend to adopt in my dotage. I wonder how the dogs in Iraq are doing and if there's a rescue group for them.

But mostly I wonder what's going on inside George's little head and inside the heads of all the other dogs I meet. And I believe it is that mystery that is the dog person's raison d'être.

For me, it's a case of Georgie on my mind.

THE COMING OF GEORGE

The dog was created specially for children. He is the god of frolic.

— Henry Ward Beecher

Trying to remember life before George is like trying to remember life before children or marriage. The details are crystalline, but the essence, the true feeling of what it was like to be the person you once were, is irretrievable. The decision to get a dog, like so many momentous decisions in my life, was reached when I wasn't exactly concentrating. I mean I knew what was going on, I just thought that if I nodded and made agreeable sounds nothing would actually happen. This is exactly what I thought before I got married and before we had a kid. You would think experience would . . . oh, never mind.

My earliest dog awareness was deeply entwined with my desire for a Dutch door. A Dutch door is a door sliced in half horizontally, so that you can open just the top for friendly chats with neighbors or to take the mail from the friendly postman. You can open just the bottom to demonstrate dance steps or expose yourself. Spring Byington opened one at the start of *December Bride*. All the kitchen sets of the happy family TV shows of the 1950s — *Ozzie and Harriet*, *Father Knows Best*, *The Life of Riley* — had Dutch doors. Or if they didn't, they should have. Since you are not likely to see a Dutch door in a New York City apartment, they were exotic to me.

But one set of family friends had a Dutch door in the kitchen. They lived in what I thought was the country (actually Yonkers), and they had a cocker spaniel named Corky, whom I sat with and petted until he got bored or hungry and trotted off. For me, dogs and Dutch doors were such stuff as dreams are made of. I saw both mostly on television.

New Yorkers grow up skilled in the art of ignoring what they don't need to attend to, so I managed to remain largely oblivious to dogs for years, except to deplore when I stepped in "the good luck." In college, I shared my first-ever apartment with Humpin' Humphrey, a roommate's dog who spent most of his days confined to the bedroom so he wouldn't eat the garbage. By the time one of us got home to let him out, Humph was so excited that he'd ejaculate on the lucky liberator's shoes.

No one has been that happy to see me since, but Humphrey did not inspire dog hunger. Nor did Finnegan the Flatulent, a venerable sort-of Irish setter with whom I shared a friend's sofa in Los Angeles for much too long. Then there was the upstairs neighbor's dog in my first postgraduate apartment. She always seemed to be pacing when I was trying to sleep. So I left the neighbor a note asking her to please keep her dog from walking around late at night. Keep the dog from walking around at night? What was I thinking?

Despite this dismal track record, my wife and I proceeded. We pored over lush dog magazines, browsed Web sites, consulted our dog-owning friends, and grimly weighed the moral implications of breeder dog versus shelter dog. For someone with my limited experience and knowledge of the canine race, the range of sizes and shapes was a revelation. The American Kennel Club currently acknowledges 146 breeds, but most estimates of extant breeds hover between three and four hundred. Desmond Morris, in his encyclopedic *Dogs*, describes a thousand, including a few that have become extinct and designer blends like the peekapoo and the Labrahuahua (not a typo). He also lists breeds for which documentation is sketchy, such as the jelly hound and the Magellanic, a breed registered at the London Zoo in 1833 and never heard of again.

For a while I was mad for any breed I'd never heard of: komondor, East Siberian laika, puli, Havanese, and hovawart. Did you know that a spinone Italiano is not a dessert? That the plural of komondor is komondorok? Why not walk the only McNab, Schapendoes, or podengo in Brooklyn? How much more complicated can it be than walking a Tom-Dick-or-Harry dog? It's not like owning an Alfa Romeo, where you have to track down a mechanic with an unlisted number and then genuflect at his feet to get your car repaired.

I felt free to entertain these fantasies because I knew we wouldn't be getting some dopey, pricey pedigree dog. Why should we, with all the perfectly nice and needy dogs on proverbial death row?

Fall approached and our deliberations grew more serious. My wife and I discovered a mutual fondness for dachshunds, but I vetoed the idea on learning they're prone to back trouble. As a back pain sufferer myself, I didn't want to risk diluting the sympathy stream. Our son has allergies, so shedding was an issue; we needed to get a dog with hair, not fur, or maybe it's the other way around. Some breeds, like poodles and bichon frises, are not merely nonshedding, they are hypoallergenic and machine washable.

We looked at dogs for adoption on the Web, figuring we'd go to a shelter or two once we got a better idea of what to expect. Frankly, I didn't relish the idea of visiting a place full of dogs yearning to get out, and my reluctance grew when we learned that the available dogs in our area seemed to fall into three different groups: scary, slope-backed German shepherd mixes; brawny, slit-eyed bull terriers resembling acid-washed versions of the one George C. Scott stomped around with in *Patton*; and a surprising number of fat, elderly Chihuahuas.

Turns out that in pet selection, as in so much else in life, both looks and size count. I realized that a big dog, no matter how appealing in the abstract, was out of the question, largely because big dogs are anything but abstract. The thought of picking up after any animal was unpleasant enough. Cleaning up after a Neapolitan mastiff would be a deal breaker. Equally unacceptable was a Blender Dog, a breed grouping invented by my wife and me that encompasses the itty-bitty dogs favored by the likes of Joan Rivers and Paris Hilton. They are called Blender Dogs because some people, though certainly not you or me, cannot look at them without free-associating to the puree buttons on their Osterizers.

Not that I share the widespread disrespect for little dogs, especially little dogs that are not working dogs, as if the reason most folks get pets is to help with the herding. A neighbor of ours calls little dogs "footballs"; his family owns a pug, by the way, which he doesn't even consider a dog. "It's a cat," he says. "A black lab, that's a dog." Even now that I'm a regular on the local dog-walking circuit, it's clear that the big-dog people don't consider me quite as *serious* a dog person as they are, with their big, swinging . . . dogs. Well, as David Frei, Westminster's chief *tummler*, once reminded the television audience, "Nobody ever has to apologize for being a fan of the little dogs."

Damn tootin'. Companion dogs have been around at least as long as dogs bred to hunt, track, herd, fight, etc. The idea that they are decadent, latter-day corruptions of working breeds is just bilge.

I didn't know any of this at the time, of course, I knew only that I could not have as a pet any animal with a bigger hat size than mine, nor so small it could accidentally be sat on. And my wife realized that she wanted a dog that was nice to look at.

She recalled a dog from a Westminster telecast a couple of years earlier. She remembered it as looking "as much like a teddy bear as a dog could look." It was a stocky, shaggy thing called a Norfolk terrier. Norfolks have small litters and high infant mortality. Richard Reynolds, an American Kennel Club judge and championship breeder, told me that the Norfolk is the only breed he knows that's born with a death wish. In 2003 only 293 Norfolk puppies were registered in the United States; it's safe to assume that anybody wanting to call a dog a Norfolk registered it. AKC registration, by the way, is construed as some sort of seal of approval for dogs, but this is not the case. Registration guarantees nothing at all about a dog except that a fee was paid by people claiming the dog is purebred. There is no club oversight of registrations, and there have been documented instances of people registering cats, themselves, and cans of tuna fish with the AKC, although these breeds have yet to achieve club recognition.

My wife left messages with the two Norfolk breeders listed in *Dogs USA*. One was Barbara Miller, who is probably the most successful Norfolk breeder in the country. Dogs from her Max-Well Kennel on Long Island win championships all the time. In 2004 the American Kennel Club named her a Breeder of the Year. She is also not one to mince words. I've learned that all telephone conversations with Barbara Miller begin the same way. She says hello, then she asks if you're calling about a dog. If you say yes, then she tells you, as she told my wife on that first phone call, to forget about it. She has no puppies, doesn't know anybody who has puppies, there is too much demand for too few puppies, there's a waiting list, and, anyway, she doesn't know you. Barbara Miller is her own velvet rope.

I was not heartbroken, particularly when we learned that the going price for Norfolk puppies was about $2,000. (Some dogs go for a lot more, I learned later. A racing greyhound went for $55,000 at auction in 2002, and Richard Reynolds told me he's heard of otterhounds selling for upward of 150K.)

There's nothing like an onerous price tag to make my egalitarian blood boil. Expensive was not what I had in mind. We're not paying big bucks for some furry status symbol, I fumed to my wife. She agreed. We'd steel ourselves to the task, drive to a shelter, and come home with a cutie.

Then the other Norfolk breeder called — Kay McKinstry from Athens, Ohio. Something about my wife's voice, she said, made her feel we'd be wonderful for her favorite puppy, George, who at just over a year was a little long in the tooth to be considered a puppy. This meant that he was already housebroken — a definite plus. George is the grandson of Ch. Buckeye Bradley, a V.I.D. in Norfolk circles. (The Ch. is for Champion.) Kay had hoped to breed him, but had no available female, aside from his mother. "I've been thinking of importing an English bitch," she said. My wife, who is English, exclaimed, "No need, here I am!" Kismet.

George isn't George's real name. Pedigree dogs have long names that invoke the creature's provenance and usually some trope of the breeder. All the puppies in a litter will be named for flowers or ice cream flavors or popular songs. Barbara Miller's dogs are named for weather phenomena like cyclones and storms. George's real name is Buckeye A Charge to Keep. Buckeye is the name of the kennel, and "A charge to keep" is a line from George W. Bush's inaugural address. When I learned this, I thought of the only notable utterance ever made by W.'s father: "This will not stand." I later told Kay that once George arrived in Brooklyn, his name became George Harrison, in honor of the Quiet Beatle. She reminded me of his AKC registration papers and I told her what I thought of AKC registrations, the tuna fish cans, and all. We changed the subject, but not for long. She said we were the first liberals she'd ever sold a dog to. I thought, it's a good thing we got him, since George is too ecumenical in outlook, too respectful of the environment, and too honest for the G.O.P.

I simply can't believe how a person of Kay's evident intelligence and integrity can believe some of the things she believes, much less support the pols she supports. She, for her part, has offered to pray for me. You see how dogs bring people together?

Christmas grew near and our Clausian plot thickened. The weekend before Christmas, my wife was suddenly "called to Washington for a special meeting." Our son suspected nothing, certainly not that she was actually slipping off to Columbus, Ohio — which, from New York, and with a dog, involves two planes each way and is more expensive and time-consuming than flying to Paris.

On my last night as a non–dog owner, I spent a quiet evening at home, feeling as if the lights were going out all across Europe. The next day I drove out to Newark Airport. My wife appeared, bearing a new piece of luggage, a black shoulder bag with mesh inserts. It was a Sherpa bag, the essential dog tote, and it was quivering. Kneeling, my wife unzipped the bag on a grassy verge abutting the parking lot. She reached in and extracted the handle of the lead, which at that time I called a leash. I still do, actually, except when I'm feeling tweedy. George cringed and shuddered quietly for a moment, then emerged, blinking and stretching and arching, as if he'd just woken up. We stood watching him as he tentatively sniffed around, peed. I took pictures.

He was a cute little thing. He never lifted his eyes to look at either of us. He took small steps; the leash was always pulled taut. George seemed to have no awareness that he was leaning into it or that he was being constrained by the collar around his neck. It was only the second time in his life he'd ever worn a collar or been on a leash. The collar came from Kay and the leash from a couple of friends who are longtime doggers. We still have them. I was in a daze, stunned that all the planning and fretting and expense had resulted in such a small creature. George allowed himself to be reboxed, which was a good thing, because getting a dog into a Sherpa bag can be much harder than getting one out.

We'd arranged with the mother of our son's friend to keep the boys occupied at her place. At home, we decorated the plastic sleeping crate we'd borrowed with a bow and some festive wrap, put the dog inside it, and called our boy home. The plan worked like a charm. He came in the door, unveiled the dog, and was so shocked he sank down on the sofa. George came over to him, ran right up my son's legs and torso, and began energetically licking his face.

In retrospect, George's behavior at this critical juncture seems to have been a striking example of emotional intelligence, and serves as counterweight to George's many more demonstrations of complete obliviousness to the dynamic of the moment. He knew what was required to secure his toehold in the home and he did it. Certainly if the dog had run up my frontispiece and begun licking my face, it wouldn't have gone nearly so well.

Over the next week or so, buyer's remorse set in. We all walked on eggshells, hopeful the experiment would work out, anxious that it wouldn't. Dog-owning friends would call to ask if we'd bonded yet. We'd smile and answer that he was really cute and a bit of a handful. Truth was, having a dog around was more work than I'd anticipated, and the payoff was unclear. Whenever I sat down to work, he'd park himself next to me and stare up urgently.

On January 4, 2002, not quite two weeks after George arrived, Kay sent us a plastic sleeping crate that had been George's. She was concerned that we did not have enough refuges for George scattered around our home. George sniffed it, whimpered, and jumped into it, pressing the whole side of his head and as much of his shoulder as he could manage into the hard plastic. Did he smell siblings? Mom? Home? Two weeks after leaving home, could he remember all that through whatever smells had survived a couple of hours in the cargo hold? Was some *Lassie Come Home* thing beginning?

George sat in the open crate bottom quietly for about a minute, and when he got out of it, he never treated the crate in that way again. For me, that was the day when George really joined the family. Or do I mean pack?

My principal relationship with George was and still is chief walker. With his rough coat and sprightly step, George was — is — a turner of heads and elicitor of smiles. I found myself explaining the difference between Norfolk and Norwich terriers several times a day. (Norfolk: adorable drop ears. Norwich: foxlike prick ears. *Vive la diff!*) Once I did it three times in one block. Here was a community of interest altogether unfamiliar to me, hidden in plain sight. But it was a community in which I felt woefully unprepared to participate. Once, after a guy with a little flat-faced dog admired George, I thought I'd return the compliment by saying something nice about his dog. "Nice French bulldog you've got," I said with complete assurance. The man looked at me as if I were the village idiot. "It's a BT," he replied. I stared at him as he strolled on, thinking "Bacon and tomato?"

In general, though, I've found that dog

people are eager to bond with others of their kind, sometimes when you least expect it. A couple of months after George's arrival, my wife and I celebrated our anniversary by ordering takeout from the fanciest and most expensive Italian restaurant in the nabe. The food was delivered by a middle-aged man in one of those double-breasted white restaurant jackets, as if he were a waiter, or at any rate grander than a delivery guy. George, of course, barked furiously at him, stopping only when I picked up the Rattle of Justice (see page 113) and shook it. Usually a stranger confronted by a forcefully barking dog, even a small dog, betrays a little anxiety, but not this guy.

"Don't worry about it," he said. "I've got a little rat terrier and he's just the same. I call him a rat *terror.* My other dog weighs about sixty pounds and she's scared of the terrier. She's a shepherd-greyhound mix with that sweet gentle greyhound character. She'll come right up to you and lean in against you."

I wondered if the wild mushroom cream sauce was congealing on the tagliatelle yet.

"How many dogs do you have?" my wife asked.

"Just the two. I had a third but she died in June. She was fifteen, a big shepherd

39

mutt of some kind. I found her tied to a lamppost and I named her Fannie, in honor of the only dog buried in Green-Wood Cemetery."

"Really?" I piped.

"O yeah, it belonged to the guy who invented the sewing machine. Elijah . . . Elias . . ."

"Howe," my wife said. How does she know these things? "Elias Howe, Jr."

"That's the guy. And I looked down and I noticed all the stones were modest, with just the names and dates of the people buried there. But I got to this small stone, and it said TO FANNIE, and then there were these lines and they went like this:

Only a dog, do you say, Sir Critic?
Only a dog, but as truth I prize
The truest love I have won in living
Lay in the deeps of her limpid eyes

"That's great," I bleated, but he rolled on.

Neither frosts of the winters, nor heat
   of the summer
Could make her fail if my footsteps led
And memory holds in its treasure casket
The name of my darling who lieth dead.

40

A hush fell over the vestibule. Then my wife said, *"Well . . ."*

"So I started crying and all, and later, when I had the chance, I thought I'd honor the dog . . ."

"Do you take credit cards?" I asked.

"Sorry?"

Oi, brave new world, I thought.

2. basic systems

OMNIVOROUS GEORGE

*Dog Feels Below Par after Eating
28 Golf Balls*

— Reuters headline, April 23, 2004

I often wonder how George, who weighs a little more than fifteen pounds, much of which is fur or maybe hair, can exert enough sudden force from his end of the leash to dislocate my shoulder. The objects of desire behind these overweening acts of torque include gum stuck to the sidewalk, old pizza crusts, soggy bagel halves, and mysterious stinky plastic bags filled with you-don't-want-to-know. Once I caught him eating a black shiny thing that could have been a cigar butt, but on closer inspection turned out to be a dead bird. It wasn't just dead, in fact, it was putrid.

I admonished my unrepentant charge. "George! People are going to think I don't feed you."

I do feed him, of course — a quarter cup of kibble twice a day, the second serving topped with a foul-smelling powder the color of turmeric that is apparently good for George's fur (hair?) and that we call cheese. His basic treat is a small biscuit that is not merely unavailable in New York City, but utterly unknown. There isn't even a place that will special-order it for you. I buy twenty-five-pound boxes of them from Nunn-Better, a milling company in Indiana with a handsome Web site, but no online billing, so I send them a check and they wait until it clears before sending off the biscuits. It is a quaint and time-consuming process, but not burdensome, because twenty-five pounds of dog biscuits lasts a long time, even when you're as profligate with them as we are, not only with George but with our many other dog friends.

One of the great commonalities shared by dogs and humans is that neither knows what's good for them in the food department. Dogs have a better excuse than we do. They literally don't know, because they can't read or speak or grasp concepts like the dual nature, both good and bad, of cholesterol. People, on the other hand, don't know what's good for them because they are idiots who don't want to know what they know. Both species' eating problems are consequences of dietary complacency.

Neither dogs nor people are terribly discriminating about what they're eating when they really, really want to eat, but dogs take it further than we do. A lot further. Consider these tales of canine gluttony:

The day my Atlanta friend Steve picked up his dog from a shelter, she ate a nail and required emergency surgery.

A friend of my wife's boarded her dog with a friend because she had to leave town. The dog ate a ham that had been left out on the kitchen counter and died.

A couple of Decembers ago, another friend brought her sweet, reserved rottweiler to the vet, because she'd been throwing up in the night. The vet checked the dog out, found nothing wrong, asked if my friend had brought the dog to any Christmas parties and if she had a tree at home, and then said, "We get a lot of vomiting dogs this time of year. It's puking season. Some of the vomit is red and green."

George has yet to eat either hardware or more than his body weight in one sitting, but he has woken up in the middle of the night vomiting. What he produced was not, if memory serves, holiday-themed. The hour was late and we were all half asleep, so we sponged down the blanket and put it in the laundry basket and put out dry bedding for his cushion. He drank some water from his bowl, ensconced himself, and, sometime later in the night, puked some more. In the cold light of day, we could see what the problem was. He'd eaten a rubber insole from one of my shoes.

As Bill Clinton might say, it all depends on what you mean by "food."

I do not claim to have a sophisticated palate, but I cannot imagine a circumstance in which I would find my insole edible. By way of contrast, I'm willing to bet plenty that George ate it with relish, brio, gusto, and zest just as, on another night, he ate a duck-fat-sodden oven mitt.

The reason is that George and I have thoroughly different ideas of food. To me, a rubber entity that spends its days in close proximity to my feet is not and can never be food, end of story. But for George, food is a fluid concept that can, and frequently does, include the unlikeliest things. Happily, eating excrement is not really his scene, which is more than I can say for some dogs I could mention, though rabbit pellets and horse apples have both provoked his interest. Thank goodness we're not around them much.

George's appetite provides us with a ready reward for training, but it also requires us to keep an eye out for him, because he will scarf down things that are bad for him, such as free-range prescription drugs, chocolate, or chicken bones, which are pliable when raw but brittle and splintery when cooked. If your dog manages to ingest one, as George has on several occasions, you spend the next few hours worrying if a shard is going to skewer some delicate innard.

If animals ate so indiscriminately in the wild, they would become extinct. Dogs in homes, however, don't have to worry about eating themselves to death. They have us.

I don't mean to suggest that all dogs are crazy to eat. I'm sure there are fussy dogs, picky dogs, and dogs who stop eating when they've had enough and not just eat and eat until they get sick. I have heard of such dogs, just as I have heard of dogs who can bark Sondheim tunes from the bottom of a swimming pool. I have just never seen one. Wanting to eat anything and everything is, as far as I can see, a natural part of the canine condition.

George's kibble and his biscuits are the same brands that Kaye McKinstry feeds her dogs and that Kay's daughter, who breeds golden retrievers, feeds hers. The kibble is high grade, made in small batches by humble craftsfolk using chickens and lambs raised lovingly on sweet old-fashioned family farms and organic grains that are grown hydroponically in Middle Earth, or maybe it's the Middle West. It is highly rated in the *Whole Dog Journal*, whose testing procedures make *Consumer Reports* seem like the Yale admissions committee that waived in Dubya. I have used other dry foods with names like Wellness, Goodness, or Enlightened Pet Owner. On a few occasions, when we've run out and feeding time is nigh, I've run around the corner and bought whatever mass-market dog food I can find, which is surely not made by elves. George eats it all with inevitable enthusiasm, which reminds me of the joke about the guy who fed his dog boiled greens. The guy's friend says his own dog wouldn't eat greens, and the guy says, "Neither would mine for the first two weeks." Sure, George eats cheap kibble with zest. He eats everything with zest. Zesty is the only gear he has.

We are fortunate. Not all dogs are so flexible. A vet told me that miniature schnauzers suffer digestive problems if they don't eat exactly the same thing at exactly the same time daily. Given that they are the only member of the terrier group whose roots are in Germany rather than Britain, I suppose it makes sense that they would be more punctual, but neither standard nor giant schnauzers are similarly time-sensitive, so the only firm conclusion we can draw is that it's probably a good thing we don't have a miniature schnauzer.

The question of what to feed our dogs is fervently and eternally debated in the Dog World. Breeders and veterinarians who recommend good-quality dry food as the basis of a dog's diet do so because assembling a balanced canine diet isn't easy, although dogs flourished long before the first commercial dog food, a biscuit concocted by an American named James Spratt, appeared around 1860 in England. Canned horse meat, presumably for dogs, appeared in stores after World War I. But from the dawn of animal domestication until the end of World War II, most dogs lived on scraps and scavenging.

But by 1945 the country had all sorts of new food processing technologies as well as massive manufacturing capacity. By the 1950s, commercial dog food, prepackaged cake mixes, and convenience foods of every stripe had come to market. Both human and canine prepared foods were promoted in the same way: by emphasizing the difficulty and unpredictability of home food preparation. This is a much easier case to make for human food, but harder for scraps, which you wouldn't think would take much effort. However, many dog foods claimed to be *scientifically formulated* to satisfy all of a dog's nutritional requirements.

Of course, most dog food isn't formulated to do much more than turn a profit from various Upton Sinclairish ingredients, including recycled restaurant grease and "meat and bone meal," a euphemism for what's left from animals slaughtered for human consumption. Meat and bone meal can include lungs, blood, feathers, ligaments, and brains. Some dog foods contain fuel oil, kerosene, peanut husks, fat stabilizers, and lead, and we haven't even gotten to the chemicals and preservatives yet. It's no wonder plenty of dog people think table scraps are preferable.

Some go further than scraps. Barbara Miller, the Norfolk breeder, makes a stew every other day with fresh beef or chicken, garlic, and a few herbs. Every third day she simmers baby carrots, reserving the nutrient-filled carrot broth to moisten the morning kibble, which is served with a tablespoon of cottage cheese or yogurt, a hard-boiled egg, brewer's yeast, multivitamins, wheat germ, and vitamin B complex. No less painstaking is my friend Jerome Vitucci, who has raised and cared for a long line of street dogs. He prepares a sort of organic mush for Sweetie, a pretty shepherd-greyhound mix (we think) and her frequent visitor, a noisy Pomeranian named Bruno. Jerome mixes equal parts of meat, vegetable, and rice, which is the most digestible grain for dogs, cooks it all together with a little broth and seasoning, and stockpiles it. After he's put up a batch, his freezer is a solid wall of little plastic tubs.

Jerome's opposition to processed dog food is vehement. He insists that a kibble diet is like making a human dine on cereal for life. It's an endless conversation, especially when Jerome gets going on the natural state of dogs. Once, in an attempt to justify George's diet, I made the mistake of showing him one of the Nunn-Better biscuits I carry in case I meet a dog I want to impress. He took it from me and brandished it.

"What do you think George would eat if he were on his own? Do you think he'd eat this? No, baby, he'd eat meat, flesh and bone. Why do you think just because George eats it, he likes it?"

"Jerome, George is not a discriminating eater," I replied. "He's eaten rotting food, he eats horse shit. Napkins are a big favorite. He's always eaten kibble. It must be what he knows as food."

"Yeah? Try serving it next to a piece of steak and see which one he goes for." Then Jerome looked disdainfully at the biscuit in his hand. "It's not natural," he said, biting off half and chewing determinedly. "It's like eating sand. Sand with lots of salt in it." Then he held the other half out to me. "Do me a favor, would you, just taste a little piece."

I don't want to do that.

Sweetie's diet is easier to maintain than the BARF diet. BARF is an acronym for bones and raw food. Putting together a healthy balance of these items for George is more effort than I am willing to expend for my whole family, and I am a person who likes to cook. Of course the diet has its loyal adherents. When you think about how crazy people get about their own diets, it's no wonder that figuring out what to feed the dog drives them mad. Take, for example, Vic (not his real name).

"Conformation is strength," said Vic assertively. "The rest is conditioning and feeding." He paused, as if waiting for someone to disagree with him, but not a peep was heard from our little group, standing in a rough semicircle by the side of an oval racing track in a bosky New Jersey suburb. We were there for a day of oval-course races sponsored by the Garden State Sighthound Association.

Sighthounds (or gazehounds or windhounds) track prey visually, running it down and either killing it or securing it until the human hunter arrives. Dogs who use their sensitive noses to track prey, such as bassets and bloodhounds, are called scenthounds and are usually slower, sturdier, and lower to the ground than the lithe sighthounds. Most of the dogs running this day were whippets, but there were plenty of greyhounds and a few basenjis and Rhodesian ridgebacks, as well.

Vic's dog, an incredibly buff whippet, was under twelve months of age and thus too young to race, but already avid. She was leaning into her extra-wide, non-choking Martindale collar with all the considerable force of her bulging hindquarters, which resembled Arnold Schwarzenegger's biceps, except that where Arnold's head would be, there was a fundament. Vic, on the other hand, was not trim. He was obese and unkempt, clad in generously sized terry-cloth stretch pants and an equally voluminous velour pullover whose deep, rich earth-tone color was set off by a profuse scattering of whippet hairs. Big squishy boots that looked as if they'd never seen a tin of polish completed the ensemble.

Vic continued to dilate on the subject of his dog's diet. "I get him Nature's Variety. It's organic and it's made in Iowa or someplace like that. I get the frozen kind, but there's also freeze-dried, which is very convenient, but you pay for that. Into that I mix a little yogurt and cottage cheese, and just try finding organic cottage cheese! And I also put in some fresh tripe and a little liver, but not too much because that'll give a dog the drizzles like you wouldn't believe."

This was getting to be too much information for me, but nobody else seemed put off, and Vic went on. "The food is so expensive that I figure if he doesn't eat it I will."

No one actually said, "We thought you did," but several of us looked down and pursed our lips in a way that suggested we'd all had the same notion more or less simultaneously. I always think of Vic and his dog when I hear the claim that people look like their dogs. It may be true, but only up to a point. Sometimes the dog represents an aspiration, or a dream. Sometimes a person should be so lucky as to look like his dog. I include myself as well as Vic in that assessment.

It's safe to say that our family will not be switching George to the BARF diet or the tripe and organic cottage cheese diet anytime soon. I intend to try Jerome's mush as soon as I can free up a large pot and three hundred little plastic containers. Until then, what's good enough for George's breeder is good enough for me. We throw in the old tiny leftover from time to time, but I'm not going to be more careful about George's diet than my own, which, though rich in good things like dark green vegetables, caffeine, and bananas, is mostly a matter of happenstance, not design.

Besides, much of the debate over what to feed dogs turns on interpreting canine behavior in human terms. It makes sense, for example, that dogs would want variety in their diets, given their sensitive noses and consequent sense of taste. But then you'd think dogs would get tired of playing Frisbee or fetch, and plenty of 'em don't. George's enthusiasm for food has never been diminished by anything other than illness, and certainly not by sameness. Would variety make him even more ravenous?

The BARF and real-food people, though, have the power of moral suasion, especially once you start pondering the conspiracy theory that all commercial dog food produces a firmer stool than real food. They put stuff in the food to produce that firmer stool, which is easier for humans to handle, but not necessarily for canines.

But wait. Isn't firm stool considered a sign of good health? Wasn't that one of the big deals about macrobiotics?

Not necessarily, it turns out. Firm stool can be a sign of too much beet pulp in the kibble. Is that so bad?

An online nutritionist called The Great Dane Lady doesn't think so, but the *Whole Dog Journal* does, sort of. It's baffling, I tell you, baffling.

So I strive to feed George responsibly, and I am dismayed by signs of incipient portliness, which even the breed description says we must expect, though there it's called "stoutness." For a few weeks once when he was sick and not eating well, we mixed bits of chicken breast, rice, and cheese into his kibble. As he felt better, he began cherry-picking the good stuff and leaving the kibble. Gradually we phased it out, but not without some persistent pouting on his part.

In *The New Work of Dogs*, Jon Katz suggests to a trainer that his dog would never recover if something were to happen to him. The trainer says that with a couple of pounds of beef liver and a week or so, the dog would forget Katz had ever walked the earth. Nothing highlights the power imbalance between man and man's best friend more than food. But even if a dog's vaunted loyalty and devotion are bought with food, shelter, and care, how different is that from the way that human bonds form? I remember looking down on my son when he was only a few weeks old and couldn't turn over, from back to front or front to back. You could lay him on the bed on his back, take a phone call, get a drink of water, read a magazine, and he'd still be there when you got back. That, I thought, is the balance of power in a nutshell. And the first time he turned over without assistance, I thought it's just a matter of time before he asks to borrow the car.

Do dogs really offer "unconditional love"? I believe we should reserve judgment on that until dogs are able to fill their food bowls themselves. Conditioning dogs to eat what you give them is a reminder that you and your best buddy aren't exactly equals.

POO CORNER

"Then there was shit."

— Edwin G. Burrows and Mike Wallace, *Gotham: A History of New York City to 1898*

Anticipating your first dog is much like anticipating your first child: Thoughts of poo are uppermost. I assumed that the specter of picking up after a dog would be of little moment to a couple who have reared a child and also regularly cleaned a tank too small for the turtles occupying it, which I can assure you is no picnic. I had the added experience of boarding a friend's cat for two weeks in the 1970s. Unfortunately, all this valuable life experience provided little succor.

And so we laid in enough Nature's Miracle, the fluid that deodorizes as it cleans, cleans as it deodorizes, to last us through a nuclear winter of potty issues. Our minds told us that elimination is just a minor detail in the larger bliss of animal companionship, but our hearts went "Eww."

At least he's small, my wife assured us hollowly. How often can a little dog need to go, she asked her friend whose parents were breeders and who grew up cleaning out kennels. Figure two or three times per day, the friend advised, and my wife exclaimed, "Three? I don't know anyone who goes that often!"

But dogs do have to go, and go often. It is a subject discussed without inhibition in any venue where people gather with their dogs. In the Dog World we assume that everyone is interested in our dogs' digestive profiles and are eager to discuss, share information, and commiserate.

And we're right. Once I was in the park with George when I encountered a stocky man with an Australian accent and three big mixes. As soon as I was within earshot, he started talking. "I offered to take my friends' dog for a walk today, and it's pooed three times. I'm running out of bags!" I smiled sympathetically. "She's a sweet dog, but they don't take her out enough; no wonder she's got all those bowel problems."

We nodded ruefully, and I won the Aussie's friendship by producing a spare bag.

Since George came to us already housebroken, my interest in toileting approaches has a more academic than practical edge. My friend Steve's dog will pee on command, a neat trick I have no plans to teach George, possibly because every time I've been commanded to pee, usually in a doctor's office, clenching has ensued, and I'll be damned if I'm doing that to George. Besides, George is no dilly-dallyer.

Steve has another friend who has taught his dog to do the other thing on command. Since the dog is a German shepherd named Eric, the command is "Erich, *sheiss!*" This dog has had shutzhund training, a rigorous practice that combines tracking, obedience, agility, and protection. Puppies suited for shutzhund training "must be more confident, more competitive, more alert, and much more aggressive than the normal companion puppy," according to *The Art of Raising a Puppy* by the Monks of New Skete, who breed and train German shepherds in upstate New York and have written two bestselling books about their methods.

Now, I am the sort of person who will never buy a VW, even though I don't suppose they're even made in Germany anymore. Teutonic efficiency just gives me the willies, but that's not the only reason crapping on command seems to me a nasty imposition. I hate to be rushed; why wouldn't George? At least he doesn't start reading and lose all track of time.

Still, Eric's treatment is less disturbing than a technique described in a book called *Smarter Than You Think* by Paul Loeb and Suzanne Hlavacek. The underlying assumption here is that your dog needs to stop wasting your time already and go. To speed that process, you take a match and stick it up your dog's bum for a minute or two and then back away. At least he recommends cardboard matches, though if one doesn't work, you're supposed to use two or three.

Even assuming George would allow that to happen without a struggle or at least considerable umbrage, I would have to be in one hell of a hurry to try such a thing.

Poo and the city are an old story. Ever since its earliest days as a tidy Dutch port, New York has been a place where shit happens. In the nineteenth century much of it came from horses, the main mode of transportation of the age, as well as pigs, a long-time urban adaptee and high-volume excreta producer. New York contained slaughterhouses, pig farms, cattle pens. In 1854 there were 22,500 horses pulling public vehicles. That doesn't include horses pulling private conveyances. Lack of a decent sewer system and ad hoc plumbing arrangements in most homes meant plenty of human waste joined the mix. The streets of Olde New York ran with the feces of the species.

Concern for public health expressed itself in gruesome ways. After a cholera epidemic in 1849, police flushed pigs from city dwellings and drove them north, while municipal bounties inspired the slaughter of 3,520 stray dogs in the street, most of them killed by club-wielding boys.

By the 1950s New Yorkers had developed sufficiently refined sensibilities to support a law against excessive horn blowing, an early attempt to deal with noise pollution. But it was not until 1978 that New Yorkers addressed another kind of pollution.

The Pooper Scooper law went into effect on August 1, 1978. It was a state law, but since it applied only to cities of 400,000 or more, Buffalo and New York were the only municipalities affected, and Buffalo later wriggled out by claiming its population was less than 400,000. It was a big-city law, and Mayor of New York Ed Koch rigorously enforced it. "It was a good law. Anybody who's ever stepped in it thinks it's a good law," he says.

But at the time of its passage, there were protests and complaints. Dog owners claimed that it was their dogs' natural right to relieve themselves wherever and whenever they wished. I remember this well, because at the time I was one of the many nondog people who dreaded the swampy summer months and to this day avoid shoes with deeply treaded soles.

According to the Environmental Protection Department at the time, New York's roughly 1,100,000 dogs were leaving 250,000 pounds of feces and 100,000 gallons of urine on city streets and parks every day.

Who do you suppose calculated these statistics? Using what raw data, if you'll pardon the expression? The numbers above come from a *Newsday* archive. No current New York agency, city or state, currently maintains figures on dog waste. A 2001 report on New York City's "solid waste stream" provides estimates for such materials as single-use cameras (23.8 tons) and milk cartons (15.08 tons), but no numbers at all for our good luck tonnage.

A Parisian government Web site, on the other hand, estimates that the city's 200,000 dogs produce 16 tons of poo per day. (In 1995 the *New York Times* reported that the City of Light leased seventy motor scooters ["caninettes"] to vacuum dog waste from sidewalks at a taxpayer cost of about $8.4 million a year. It also reported that an average of 650 Parisians a year end up hospitalized or with broken limbs after slipping on shitty sidewalks.) The Victorian Litter Action Alliance maintains that the 900,000 dogs in Victoria, an Australian province, produce 90 tons of poo per day. DEFRA, the U.K.'s Department of Environment, Food and Rural Affairs, puts the British dog population at approximately 6.8 million, producing 900 tons of excrement a day. The DEFRA Web site uses these formidable statistics to purvey useful advice on exactly how to pick up after your dog: "Simply place a bag over the dog mess and lift it whilst pulling the bag downwards." Whilst!

After running the stats through the old calculator a few dozen times, I got my son to do the math. Here's the breakout of poo production per dog, per day, rounded to two places:

New York City dogs in 1978: .23 lb.
Parisian dogs (current): .16 lb.
Victoria (Aus.) dogs (current): .20 lb.
British dogs (current): .26 lb.

Questions arise: Do French dogs have their own paradox? How come they produce so much less *merde* than the other dogs? Is it the red wine in their kibble?

More important, who's kidding who? You don't have to be a Dog Worlder to know these numbers are wack. The only dogs that produce a quarter pound of poo a day are eating too little fiber. George, not a big guy, produces more than that, not that I'm bragging. Labs and retrievers and standard poodles, forget it.

So why do these agencies of widely varied governments go to the trouble of cooking numbers in such a way as to suggest that their dog populations are wildly constipated? I suspect it is a fig leaf for the general difficulty of governments to get people to pick up after their pets.

In Paris and Rome, the penalty for failure to scoop comes to about a hundred dollars. Natives of both cities tell me enforcement is lax. In Rome, you can be fined even more if you're caught walking your dog without poop-scooping tools, such as bags or a shovel, with you. In effect, the law can punish you for a crime you have not yet committed, just like in *Minority Report* or the Patriot Act.

The fine in New York for failure to scoop tops out at $100, and the city government wants you to know that it's vigorously enforced. To that end, an archival photo of a police officer writing a ticket to an errant, nonscooping dog walker resides in perpetuity on the New York Government Web site. (See for yourself at http://www.nyc.gov/html/dos/html/annual98/html/ar98t1302.html.)

The Pooper Scooper law is one of the few laws in New York that enjoys active support from the citizenry, even unto enforcement. "When I walk down the street and my Stella starts to prepare herself," a neighbor laments, "all eyes on the street are on me. One day I'm going to forget a bag and someone will make a citizen's arrest."

And that arrest would be justified. Call it a matter of values. Picking up the dog's business is the inalienable obligation of the urban dog person. New Yorkers understand this and that is why so many of us favor the death penalty for poop law violators, preferably by slow and painful means. When it comes to dogs, we are all vigilantes, spying on our fellows with a furtive intensity that would tickle the cockles of John Ashcroft's stony heart, assuming he hasn't had his cockles surgically removed.

While New Yorkers attack the problem in their customary hands-on way, there are other approaches. One of the oddest is Maurice Grabett's.

Among the many hundreds, possibly thousands of canine artists, booksellers, and tchotchke-mongers displaying their wares at the 2004 Crufts Dog Show in England, Maurice Grabett was probably the newest at the game. His invention, the Poochstick, had been on the market only three days. A walking stick with a difference, the Poochstick enables the user to pick up a dog's business without stooping or having any manual contact with the live good luck, even through the protective membrane of a plastic bag, which many people find distasteful in the extreme, but most reasonable dog people consider a fact of life, though that's just my opinion.

The lower third of the Poochstick is a hollow, detachable, and biodegradable "collecting capsule." You follow your dog, place the Poochstick over the offending mound or mounds, and press down. When the capsule is full, you simply throw it away. A small light hidden on the underside of the handle provides visibility when retrieving nocturnal eliminations. As of this writing, you can see and order one at www.pooch7stick.com.

Mr. Grabett's invention is a result of his frustration with the failure of the U.K.'s Fouling of Land Act of 1996. The act applies to places like tourist beaches and promenades, footpaths, pavements, picnic sites, sports grounds, pedestrian areas, and verges, whatever verges are. The initial fine is 50 p. Repeaters can be prosecuted through the Magistrate's Court, where a maximum fine of £1,000 can be imposed. Mr. Grabett told me he has neither seen nor heard of anyone fined under the law.

Although I admire Mr. Grabett's energy and inventiveness, his solution to one of the industrialized world's enduring quality of life issues is fraught with problems. First of all, how do you get the end product to go up into the removable capsule? It doesn't always want to do that. How do you detach the detachable shell without risk of poo contact? Do you have to use a fresh capsule for every walk? That could get expensive. If they're reusable, where do you keep them until they're full? It's just a worrisome product, though I wish Mr. Grabett luck with it.

He will need luck. He enters a crowded field. Here are some of the products with which the Poochstick, if it makes it to these shores, will compete: "The Jaw" One Handed Black Pooper Scooper, Four Paws Spring Action Scooper, Four Paws Scissors Style Sanitary Pooper Scooper, Four Paws Doggie Doo Bags ("Tie handles on bag and you're done!"), Handy Doody Scoop, and the Kwik Pik Scooper.

Nelson's Backyard, a square of real grass growing on a little movable platform, is aimed at a niche market: small dogs who live in high-rises. Just put the square on the terrace (or somewhere) and train the dog to go there.

The Dog Diaper is just what it says it is, and though its Web site contains an impassioned plea for the environmental consequences of other forms of poo disposal and a video clip of an embarrassed-looking

Doberman prancing around with one on, I will not be touching one of them with a ten-foot pole, and I know I speak for George as well. But I am taken with the Bramton Outright "Pee Post" Yard Stake, a training device that claims to provide "the charming trompe l'oeil effect of having a municipal fire hydrant in your yard."

There are also, of course, plenty of services that will, for a price, come into your home or your yard and pick up after your dog for you. At the home page of aPaws, the Association of Professional Animal Waste Specialists, you can find member companies in a state-by-state directory whose names demonstrate once again that the Dog World is full of people who like puns, plays on words, and, in general, the sort of humor that makes my fillings hurt. Here is contact information for Yucko's Pooper Scooper Service (#1 in St. Louis for Turd-Herding!), Doggie Doo Not, When Doody Calls, In the Line of Dooty (note spelling variants), Entre-Manure, Dirty Work, Poop Masters, We Do Doo Doo, and more.

Such services are particularly popular in the suburbs, where slothful dog owners are wont to let their dogs out into their yards, from whence the shit is picked up once a week or so. What happens in between visits is something I prefer not to dwell on, but the arrangement would certainly put a damper on your use and general enjoyment of the yard. In a word, ick. This custom is another excellent reason why you will never catch me living in a suburb.

Some rules are meant to be broken, of course, and no one knows that better than George. Though our little garden is not one of his regular unloading zones, sometimes he just can't resist, especially if I'm dithering before his morning walk. Since my wife is the gardener in the family, she usually discovers George's souvenirs before I do, which led her to leave me this note last Father's Day: *"I picked up the poo in the garden! xxx."*

SPECIAL FEATURE: HOW TO PICK UP AFTER YOUR DOG

I hate to be judgmental, but anybody who carries around any sort of widget so as not to have to touch the bag that holds the poo is an idiot. Such gimcracks lead to excessive fussing, which is both unseemly and can lead to accidents. To clean up effectively after your dog with a modicum of grace and flair, bend from the hips, not the waist, and, with hand covered by a suitably impervious membrane, pick the stuff up.

Form is everything here. Don't think about what you're hefting, think about how you look when you're hefting it. You'd be surprised how many people smile airily at the moment of retrieval, as if to say "Isn't this fun?"

Write this down: The idea is not to look as if you're having a great time. The idea is to look like a smooth, efficient, and responsible citizen of the earth and not one to get all freaked out by a perfectly natural function.

Preparation, of course, is key. I never carry fewer than two plastic bags when I walk George, because sometimes he does a little reprise, especially after a long walk. I keep them tucked away out of sight. Nothing looks worse than plastic bags sticking out of pockets. Everybody knows why you're out there; why advertise? Worse still is tucking them under the belt of one's fanny pack, in itself a style malfeasance that should carry jail time. Worst of all are those callous doggers who tuck their bags under their dogs' collars, which I believe constitutes a form of animal cruelty. Would you like to walk around with a roll of toilet paper around your neck, like a Saint Bernard toting a keg of brandy? It's undignified.

The right bag for the job is essential. Good bags are smaller than average, yet long enough to knot easily; they are opaque and have no holes. Craftsmanship is important. The organic bags that decompose are very well made. The very best are the slim blue bags the *New York Times* is delivered in. They allow for full coverage, and the extra length makes for easy knotting. Quality can be iffy. Always check your bag for holes before you go out. You do not want to be surprised at the eleventh hour. We store good bags in the Good Bag Storage Bag, right near the front door, convenient for frenzied exits.

Dogs are teaching us when we walk them. They are teaching us to stop and smell the roses or, in George's case, the Coke cans, bundled newspapers, crushed Big Gulp cups, and wads of wet cardboard. I have learned over years of accompanying George on his eliminatory quests that it is never wise to rush things. Try not to have too strict an agenda, such as getting home before your favorite show goes on or your ass freezes off. Such imperatives have little meaning to your dog. While waiting, your attitude should be neither ebullient nor embarrassed. It is a natural function, after all, and it's not as if you're the one squatting there.

Similarly, expressing distaste during the act of retrieval is unsporting, possibly hurtful to your dog, and reflects poorly on you. For goodness' sake, don't squeeze the bag or contemplate its temperature. Your attitude should be one of mildly amused stoicism, not barely contained revulsion. You never want to look impatient or fussed. I always offer praise when George leaves a tight grouping. I figure it can't hurt.

Remember that people who walk their dogs are divided into two classes: those who have been caught without a bag and those who will be. On such occasions, it is imperative to return to the scene of the crime if at all possible and make things right. That is what I've always done.

Except once. Late one night I took George out for what I'd hoped would be a quickie. It was bleak, cold, and rainy. Of course, George was delighted to be out in the wet and apparently the thought of going didn't occur for blocks. I was getting antsy.

On a deserted corner three blocks or so

from my house, George assumed the position and let loose right between the cobblestones surrounding a small tree by the curb. It was then that I realized George had a tummy upset and getting down between the cobblestones in the driving rain with my plastic bag was not going to be fun. I looked around and I realized that I knew the family in the house in front of which George had just made his mess. And I remembered the many spirited conversations that had gone on all over the nabe when the 2000 election was still up in the air. I thought about where these folks stood on that one. And George and I went home. Let *them* pick it up.

DOG NUTS

Man denies sex with Jack Russell.

— AP headline

On my way back from Crufts, the enormous British dog show, I sat across the aisle from Robert Seitz, a retired pathologist who runs a flower shop and raises borzoi, formerly know as Russian wolfhounds, on the side.

Several of his dogs had just won prizes at the show, so he was in an expansive and chatty mood. Talk turned to George; I told our tale and went into his lineage because dog show people are interested in that sort of thing. When I explained that George was simply a pet and had been fixed, Robert made a sour face and said indignantly, "How would you like it if someone did that to you?"

The fancy, as the dog show universe is called by its, um, fanciers, is all about unneutered dogs, since the whole process is supposed to be concerned with the onward march of genetic improvement. No dog can compete in the show ring without gonads that rock. But according to the Humane Society, 72 percent of owned dogs in the United States are spayed or neutered. Outside of dog shows, the only large group of unneutered dogs I've ever seen was atop the stairs leading up to the Soldiers and Sailors Monument in Fort Greene Park, Brooklyn. Standing in a loose circle were about a dozen teenage boys, each of them holding a pit bull on a leash. All the dogs were male and intact or, as some fanciers say, "entire." It was a quiet gathering, the boys strolling their dogs around and talking. The dogs looked alert but not on guard. I got the hell out of there anyway.

Some professional dog walkers balk at walking unneutered dogs. If you are buying a purebred dog for a pet, the breeder may require the dog to be neutered as a condition of sale. Some will have the animal fixed before they will release it to you.

The noisiest local stallion in these parts is an intact dachshund who barks at larger dogs and passersby like a drill sergeant. Up the block, by contrast, is a serene though all-man Lab whom George adores and whom I've never seen make an aggressive move. Whether this is because he wears a prong collar and is not in a position to make demands or because he is genuinely a mellow dude, I couldn't say. The dog is clearly not a show dog and has never been bred. I've learned from the lady of the house that the men of the house, father and son, don't see the need. I have not asked either of them their reasons. I feel awkward about asking, I think, for more or less the same probable reason the dog hasn't been fixed, some combination of identification and squeamishness.

I find the swagger of men alongside their unneutered dogs just a touch ridic. I mean, when you see a man strutting alongside a great Dane whose jiggling scrotum turns heads as he clops by, what connections are you supposed to make? Does the same gender pride exist for female owners of unspayed bitches? I wonder. Do they walk around with their animals humming "You Make Me Feel Like a Natural Woman"? I can't begin to think who to ask about this, but I have the comfort of knowing that if such a group exists, they will probably open a branch in my neighborhood.

I know of one family who bred their Dalmatian bitch with another Dalmatian, so the children could witness the miracle of life. My friend Gerry remembers the summer the bitch had her litter. "One after another came out and died. It was very depressing."

Bitches in heat can't run in races either at greyhound tracks or at the amateur events I've attended. They create too much disruptive behavior, which seems to me a clear-cut case of gender bias. I mean, whose disruptive behavior is it? It's another case of women getting penalized for men behaving badly.

A lot of dog people believe that aggression has more to do with temperament and training than hormones. It is certainly clear that neutering is no guarantee a dog will behave. I see a dog almost daily who makes that point abundantly clear.

"Digby, resist that temptation," the voice calls out, starting out in alpha mode, but rapidly rising in pitch to hysterical auntie mode. "Digby . . . Dig . . . DIG!" And the guy has to go and peel his dog off the hindquarters of the other dog, who may be annoyed or just as possibly oblivious to the desperate pumping of Digby's hips.

Digby is the most flagrant local example I know of a dog who just can't keep his groin to himself. Although fixed, he spends his off-leash time in the park coming up behind unsuspecting playmates of a wide range of sizes, shapes, and degrees of irritability. And there, on the green rolling hills of Prospect Park, he tries to do what comes naturally, or would come naturally if only. The dog is in no way vicious or out of control, except for this one tiny little problem, the humping thing.

In an informal survey conducted by myself, mounting is one of the five most annoying dog behaviors, especially among non–dog people. The others are barking at doorbells or phones, pulling on the leash (Are you reading this, George?), nipping (or even just mouthing), and begging for food. Dogs mounting other dogs is annoying enough, especially if your dog is an unwilling humpee, but people get really displeased when dogs hump them. Certainly my college roommate's dog, Humpin' Humph, and his demonstrative ways did not play well with any of the infrequent dates we brought by.

I'm happy to report that mounting is not and never has been George's scene, though jumping up is a distinct possibility if he likes you (and if it bothers you that a little dog is so pleased to see you that he puts his paws on you, then all I have to say is, get a life). But given that mounting behavior is practiced by dogs of both genders, both fixed and not fixed, I wonder what causes it. Is it a vestige of hormonal inspiration, a scrap of sexuality struggling for expression, or is the urge like a program still running in the computer of the dog's mind, or rather trying to run, even though the necessary hardware is no longer there?

At least one man believes that neutered male dogs know something is missing, and he's built a business out of dog owners who agree with him. He makes costume (family) jewelry.

"No one on this Earth had ever heard or even dreamed of testicular implants for pets until Neuticles were created," Gregg Miller, their inventor, says, and who am I to quibble? It certainly is an arresting concept, and it might never have come to be if it hadn't been for Miller's beloved bloodhound, Buck.

They lived in the country near Independence, Missouri. Buck pretty much came and went as he pleased, until he disappeared for three days, then showed up outside a farmhouse and wouldn't leave. Turns out there was a bitch in season inside. The choice was simple: Neuter Buck or put him down.

"I had always grown up with unneutered dogs," Miller told me, not quite accurately. Two of his childhood dogs were females, and the male was a dachshund whom I gather wasn't outside much. The girls, Cookie and Delilah, were spayed. "It's different with females," he protests, a shade too much. "They come in heat and they're dripping."

Buck came home from the vet a changed dog. "Buck loved his testicles," Miller recalls wistfully. "It was a big part of his daily ritual, cleaning them and what-not. When they were gone he grieved for them for about three days."

Guilt is not commonly held as a particularly productive state of mind, but for Miller, it was inspirational. Two years after

Buck's loss, in 1995, the first Neuticles were installed in a nine-month old rottweiler named Max. Since then Miller tells me there have been 147,700 neuterings with Neuticles at more than 8,500 veterinary clinics in all fifty states. (I, for one, would like to know more about the Neuticle community in Alaska, Land of Iditarod.) In 1997 NeuticalsNaturals were introduced. They're made of "marshmallow soft" solid silicone, with a more natural feel than the disconcertingly firm polypropylene of NeuticlesOriginals. Neuticles now offers models to fit cats, bulls, and horses. Miller does custom work, as well, and has produced Neuticles for prairie dogs, water buffalo, rats, and rhesus monkeys. In 2000 a California man who'd lost a testicle attempted to have a Neuticle inserted, but the FDA would not permit the procedure. Miller maintains that his product is safer than the only legal testicular implants for men, which are saline. Once you've got the hang of making synthetic testicles, apparently all you've got to worry about is sizing, not species, since testicles have a universal shape. "They're all the same," Miller says, with weary authority.

The Neuticles' pitch is an appeal to "the caring pet owner," but there's not much scientific basis to support the contention that dogs miss something or feel diminished by that something's loss. In a pamphlet, the Humane Society goes so far as to assert that "pets don't have any concept of sexual identity or ego." No sexual identity, check. No ego — they must be kidding.

There's no reason to think your dog would not appreciate Neuticles. On the other hand, there's no reason to think your dog would be the one paying for them. On the Neuticles Web site are various testimonials, including one from an English vet, who says, "I think more chaps would agree to neuter their pets if they knew about Neuticles." If you say so, Doc.

George was neutered a few days before my wife went to get him, when he was just a bit over a year old. He seems okay with it and has never humped anything.

But, as I often say in my clever paraphrase of the taxicab scene from *On the Waterfront*, George coulda been a contender. As Kay McKinstry told us, and as is clear to anyone with eyes to see, gorgeous George inherited Grandpa Bradley's good looks. Kay hoped to breed him. If a suitable bitch had come along before we did, he might have gone on to glory in the ring and at stud. So even though we had no say in the matter, we do bear some responsibility for George's missing out on a show business career and the subsequent loss of his manhood. That's one of the great things about man's relation to the rest of the Animal Kingdom. Guilt is always reasonable.

I asked Kay if she thought George might have had the right stuff to excel in the fancy. She thought he had the looks but not the temperament. I was glad to hear that, because I would hate to think we'd forced George to hide his light under a bushel. Besides, his temperament is perfect for us.

3. simple pleasures

OFF-THE-JOB TRAINING

It seemed the ordained order of things that dogs should work.

— Jack London, *The Call of the Wild*

In their long years with humans, dogs have been bred for all sorts of tasks. Rhodesian ridgebacks hunted lions. Dachshunds are purpose-built to go down holes after badgers. The Tosa Inu, a huge mastiff from Japan, earned the sobriquet "the Silent Killer" because it can fight without growling or barking or, evidently, even breathing hard. (I know of a Brooklyn Tosa who lives with a cairn terrier one-tenth her weight. Guess who runs the show?)

The most extraordinary example I know of serious breed specialization is the Nova

Scotia duck tolling retriever. Here is a dog who is, by instinct, a double agent. The toller looks foxlike, with a reddish coat and a white-tipped tail. Its M.O. is pretty foxy, too. It frolics around in a nonpredatory way near bodies of water. Waterfowl, attracted by the pastoral goings-on, come in for a closer look and to take a load off their wings. The dog retreats. There is an "uh-oh" moment, when the birds suddenly catch the drift and fly up, but it's too late, and N.R.A. members blow the birds out of the sky. With the help of paws that are webbed for just such an eventuality, the toller swims out and brings back the quarry. Seduction, betrayal, retrieval: mission accomplished by the Water Dog Who Came in from the Cold.

Dogs didn't become the utility infielders of Class Mammalia by accident. Their incredible variety is a result of breeding, not evolution. And they developed in all these diverse ways because there was diverse work for them to do. Some of this work still goes on. Farmers and ranchers use dogs, and so do mushers and therapists and security agencies and the army.

But the work of most dogs nowadays is to be pets, or animal companions, the term of the hour, and the original purposes for which they were bred just no longer obtain. The prices for ridgebacks being what they are, it's doubtful many of them are still hunting lions, and if you have a badger problem, you're likelier to call the Orkin man than unleash your weiner dog. And so a common challenge for dog people is providing stimulation for their underemployed dogs.

At the same time, breeders face the challenge of trying to ensure that their dogs actually can do what they were meant to do. The task is easier if the breed and its aficionados are not large. Before you can acquire a wirehaired pointing griffon from a breeder sanctioned by the Wirehaired Point Griffon Club of America, for example, you must agree that you will take the dog hunting, among other contractual obligations. Such commitments are rarely required when you buy a golden retriever or dachshund, though that dog will probably have papers, too.

Like most terriers, George should by rights excel at digging and catching vermin. He is a pretty formidable digger for, oh, minutes at a time. Then he gets bored. It should be noted for reasons that will become clear shortly that his digging looks absolutely adorable, all busy paws and waggly butt.

His predatory instincts, on the other hand, are nowhere. He will stare at fish in a pond and occasionally make a tentative swipe with a paw, but I think he's just trying to touch them. Maybe he's waving. He has "caught" precisely two mice in our house and while I'd like to say that's because that's all we've had, it's really because those two were already dead in traps. George ate one with customary relish, the second he extricated from the trap, took upstairs, and left on my pillow.

These behaviors, whatever they reveal about the state of George's instincts, demonstrate what is by far the Norfolk's most visible and desired quality. I am speaking of extreme cuteness, the trait that dare not speak its name. After all, the Norfolk crowd insists, Norfolks are working terriers, even if they do look like teddy bears. It is the cuteness factor, much more than George's dubious ability to catch mice, that is most appreciated by casual passersby as well as family, the latter perhaps more incessantly than we really should (our appreciation is often accompanied by edible treats, pats, rubs and more treats, and George could stand to drop a pound or two).

George has assumed, perfectly reasonably, that the mice are not part of his job description. Vermin have never been critical to George for food or diversion; you can understand why he's blasé about them.

I say there is no shame in acknowledging that most pets have lost their original occupations. Herding dogs don't herd, sporting dogs don't sport. Tibetan spaniels don't turn prayer wheels or lounge atop high walls, googly eyes peeled for intruders. Portuguese water dogs may still swim, but rarely for a living and probably less and less in Portugal, where they nearly became extinct. (But they are, at least, Portuguese in origin. Surprisingly, breed names and a breed's actual origins don't always match. Italian greyhounds aren't Italian, Australian shepherds aren't Australian, and Dalmatians have no roots in Dalmatia. On the other hand, Boston and Tibetan terriers, while hailing from Boston and Tibet respectively, are not terriers. Go figure.)

While I delight in the sheer variety of dogs, I believe there is often a gap between intention and result. It's not always clear to me that dogs are so good at their intended skill. Consider, for example, the numerous breeds developed to hunt otters, both hounds and terriers. There are all the otterhounds (black and tan, yellow-speckled), the Dandie Dinmont, Airedale, a couple of dozen in all. Otters, you would think, would be endangered. But they are not, suggesting two possibilities. Either otters were once a scourge that they are not today, or otter-hunting dogs simply have never been much good at it.

Otterhound inefficiency aside, the point is that most dogs rarely have the chance to engage in the activities their ancestors did and that their instincts, theoretically, still tell them to do, more or less. There are no lion hunts for our ridgies, no vole-a-thons for our terriers. So how do we, the stewards of our dogs, keep them busy and active, and out of our hair?

We walk them.

SUNDAYS AND THE ALL THE OTHER DAYS IN THE PARK WITH GEORGE

The trouble with dogs is that you have to walk them all the time, and the great thing about dogs is that you have to walk them all the time.

— Neighbor Aldo, currently walking Sparky

Dog walking is the central act of the urban dog person and the essential expression of the dog-human bond. It is the one activity that almost every dog and dog owner share. A city dog's life is built around walks. And now my life is built around a city dog's walks, too.

My daily routine is arranged to accommodate George's to an extent undreamed of by anyone who knows me, including my family, except for you. This is true even if I am not the one doing the walking. Before I schedule a meeting or a lunch or a doctor's appointment, I make sure George's walks are arranged. Once a moment's lapse in my vigilance forced me to miss my annual tax-time hadj to my accountant, with whom it is harder to arrange face time than with J. D. Salinger, during April anyway.

That was a mere inconvenience, solved by a little groveling and a reschedule. But there are expenses and detours that surprise me even when I see them coming. And they can be quite staggering in relation to the size of the dog. When a spiffy new print of *Lawrence of Arabia* played at the Manhattan Ziegfeld, which has one of few remaining giant movie screens around, I planned a family excursion, with dinner out afterward, so that my son could at last learn where all his dad's best impressions come from. Then I started to think about how long George would be alone, and who would feed him, and how'd he feel at home all alone as bright afternoon turned to dusk, and then evening, and I thought about George on a camel riding across the endless sands, and soon I was on the phone to Camp Dog, which is our name for a boarding kennel that George always seems incredibly eager to visit, judging by the way he hurls himself at the car window when we drive up to the place. Of course, dropping him off added a little time to our trip to the movies, and we had to pick him up the next day, but doing so enabled me to keep George's expenses for our movie under fifty bucks. It was the least I could do, after all. I mean, George would have been home alone in the neighborhood of seven or eight hours, with nothing but the entire house, buckets of toys, food, ample water bowls, and *Animal Planet* on the tube to distract him.

It's not that George hasn't been home alone for that long. He has, on more than one occasion, and he took his confinement the way any sensible being would: by curling up and going to sleep. George got a night at Camp Dog not because he couldn't have managed being cooped up for that long, but because I couldn't manage being cooped up for that long. Without access to a toilet or the ability to take a step outside, my bladder would swell up like a basketball, previously unknown allergies would kick in, and I would go insane.

George gets three to five walks a day, depending on whether he goes off with his afternoon playgroup, depending on the weather, depending on which chair he falls asleep on, depending on how much poking around he does in the garden, depending on a lot of things. I do at least two of these walks, the first and last. If I'm not handling the other walks myself, I plan who will, and when.

Minding the walk schedule isn't so much a matter of devotion as of something much more powerful: preemptive guilt, the conviction that if I mess up, something horrible will ensue, and it will be my fault. The obligation to walk the dog weighs on me, heavily at times, but the burden is lightened by the pleasure of the activity itself. Mostly. Especially in the morning.

My morning walk with George is as essential to my well-being as that first glass of juice or my habit of reading selected human interest stories from the sports page aloud to my somnolent wife, a habit she wishes I'd curtail, but that's another story. What's so great about it? Let me count the ways; I get seven, same number as the Pillars of Wisdom (see *Lawrence of Arabia*):

1. The Power of Smugness: One August morning I headed out during a torrential downpour. The street in front of my house looked like a rushing stream. George seemed too rapt by the smells on the curb even to notice the rain, which by now you could call a freshet, and peeing was clearly not on the top of his to-do list. After a few damp minutes, a familiar face appeared across the street, with four more familiar faces at the ends of their respective leashes. It was the Rainbow Coalition, four dogs of different shapes and sizes, all in ponchos and all soaking wet anyway, but no one appeared to mind. The scruffy Boston terrier seemed as usual to be setting the pace for the ridgeback and the two amiable mutts. As we neared, the human in charge and I exchanged smiles the way sports car owners used to flash their headlamps when passing on the road. "Only the true doggers are out today," she said. I blushed with pleasure. We few, we brave, we . . . doggers.

2. The Reassurance of Routine: Everyday activities provide ballast in an uncertain world. I like making sure we don't run out of milk or juice or eggs, so I check seven or eight times a day before I go grocery shopping. I like grocery shopping, so long as it doesn't involve the supermarket. I like doing laundry, so long as it doesn't involve folding. I like moving the car from one side of the street to the other on the days when alternate-side-of-the-street parking rules are in effect. (Note to evangelicals: The intricacies of New York City's alternate-side-of-the-street parking regulations are what the Beast will have you struggling to grasp for all eternity if you're not careful, so be very good in this life, especially to New Yorkers.) What I am getting at is that I am a creature of habit. Now I am a creature of George's habits, too.

3. The Thrill of Intransitive Walking: Why did the New Yorker cross the road? To get to the other side, not to have a lovely stroll. In other words, walking is the best way to get around town. It is faster than driving, nicer than the subways, and there's always something interesting to look at. That is why I, like so many of NYC's native peoples, am an inveterate walker. But, I hasten to add, I am not a walker of the footloose, I-Love-to-Go-a-Wandering type. I walk in the classic New York style, purposefully. Aimless walking without a destination, as in "taking a walk," is much more tiring than walking from point A to point B. Aimless walking at a very slow pace is the most tiring of all. After forty minutes in an airport or department store, for instance, I'm ready for a chair with good lumbar support or, failing that, a bar stool. That's what comes of the wrong kind of walking.

Dog walking is different from both walking to get somewhere and walking to take a walk. It's not that there's no destination involved. There are plenty of destinations. Each walk is an odyssey, beginning and ending at the same place, but with many stops along the way. Indeed, George has dozens of destinations when we're out walking, and that's just on our block. But from my perspective, and I suspect from George's, too, it doesn't matter much whether we turn right or left on Eighth Avenue, circle the block or stroll down the avenue and back, or just dawdle. Wherever we go, George sniffs trees and under cars. He hunts down morsels, and stares transfixed at the ominous-looking black garbage bags that decorate the sidewalks the night before garbage collection day. The ultimate destination is always the same, at home where we started. The journey is the thing.

4. *The Pleasure of Knowing the Weather:* Every morning as she leaves for work, my wife stands outside our front door and looks up at the sky. It is her weather moment, before she walks determinedly to the subway station and disappears. By the time she's home, it's dark or nearly dark. On weekdays, the weather is completely irrelevant to her except as a topic of conversation, for which purpose, of course, it can't be beat.

Most of the known world is obsessed with the weather. We anticipate it, revile it, enjoy it, or endure it. And we discuss it, ad nauseam or ad infinitum, depending on the weather.

But we do not necessarily experience it. For many, weeks can go by without any exposure to the elements lasting longer than a few minutes. You can live quite happily in the city with only the vaguest idea of what the elements are up to. Pre-George, my exposure to them often was limited to a walk to the corner for coffee and sometimes less.

To me, this is one of the joys of city life.

My idea of a good time has rarely if ever involved the great outdoors, which I personally have never found so great. I used to maintain that I wouldn't mind if the whole world was paved. I was only joking.

Since George got here, I've changed. Now not a day goes by that I am not fascinated by the abundant weather that greets me: rain, sun, wind, clouds, sleet, the whole meteorological nine yards. And it's not so bad! It's a whole new world, this place we call "outside," a world I have long suffered but rarely savored.

Now, like my wife, I stand at the top of the stoop in the morning to take in the air, the light, the sky, the precip, if any. Then I double-lock the door with one hand whilst [sic] the other grips George's leash as he flings himself down the stairs to fend off a loitering sanitation truck that has violated his personal space. As a morning routine, the walk is never less than enjoyable. Well, maybe very rarely. It's important to dress appropriately, which brings us to point number

5. *The Joy of Dressing Way, Way Down*: As I pointed out in my seminal 1995 essay, "The Brooklyn Grooming Disaster," my neighborhood is not populated by those you would call snappy dressers. In fact, you could say it is the most style-free region in the industrialized world, a black hole of fashion where dowdy meets functional with laughable results.

Don't get me wrong. I love it here. I'm a short walk from the zoo, the Botanical Garden, the Brooklyn Museum and Public Library. We have one coffee joint per adult resident, good pizza parlors, and we're a mere ten minutes by car from an excellent butcher. In my garden, I've seen a hummingbird, a raccoon, and a turtle — not all together in a group, mind you, but still impressive separately. I think Park Slope is the loveliest part of the most beautiful borough in the most exciting city in the world. But chic, au courant, elegant, soigné? Not a chance.

The causes of this local fashion vacuum go back to the 1960s, when white flight, exacerbated by the loss of the Dodgers and the waterfront, decimated the Slope, Brooklyn's former Gold Coast, leaving the historic neighborhood to the first generation of brownstone pioneers, who are now aging hippies with their dismal little ponytails and Birkenstock shoes and the lowest-numbered membership cards at the Food Co-op.

The hippies were followed by wave upon wave of baby food–encrusted young parents and a large community of flannel-shirted gals. None of these groups — bohemians, parents, and lesbians — attaches much importance to dressing for success, or to looking trendy, or even to avoid being mistaken for a homeless person. They are the root stock from whom our neighborhood's unique fashion profile evolved. In recent years an influx of Wall Streeters has created a more affluent street scene, but hardly a more stylish one. Aside from a few fashionista working women I see hard-charging to the subway in the morning and the infrequent young hipster, Park Slope is the land that pizzazz forgot. Nowhere else do so many people who could clearly afford to put themselves together so utterly neglect to do so. It's no wonder I'm so comfortable here. The last time I was finicky and self-conscious about my clothing, the Beatles were still together.

But the frowsy, frayed, down-at-the-heels Slope style — let's call it XXX-treme casual — is positively snazzy compared to what the dog people wear. Having a dog, it turns out, affords the opportunity to take slovenliness to a whole new level, and the opportunity is seized by many. Threadbare sweatpants, multiple ill-fitting layers, and nonsensically sensible shoes are the order of the day. On really cold days, I don my Michelin Man parka that leaks tiny white feathers and a brimmed woolen cap with earflaps that fold down from inside the crown, a look that got me pushed around more than once when I was a kid. Clothes are only a part of the deal. It's also important to have the right stuff.

6. *The Joy of the Right Stuff:* I don't like shopping. I buy almost everything on-line or through catalogs, and the lengths to which I'll go to avoid a brick-and-mortar store surprise even me. All bets are off, however, when looking for dog-related gear. Most of these essentials are not the sort of thing you'd think you can work up much interest about, like water bowls. One water bowl's pretty much the same as another, right? Wrong! Plastic bowls can cause dogs to lose nose pigment! At the same time, my weakness for technical clothing inappropriate for urban living has received a new lease on life. My enormous snow boots, for example, would be better suited to an Antarctic rescue mission than poop patrol in Brooklyn. I just hope I never have to run in them.

My Gore-Tex rain parka is another item I couldn't possibly have justified pre-George. It's a color the folks at L.L.Bean call teal, which is sort of a clinically depressed turquoise. It's got a hood and a formidable array of flaps, gussets, zips, and tabs, each individually adjustable. It's the sort of horror I never thought I'd own, much less wear. Now I put it on if it's just cloudy, because who wants to worry about getting soaked when you're standing around not walking during your walk? Fortunately, you don't have to look at it when it's not in use. It folds up into a little parcel not much bigger than a calzone, that is, assuming I remove the jar of Musher's Wax, for smearing on George's paws when there's ice and rock salt on the ground, from the coat pocket. I keep it there in case of sudden blizzards.

7. *The Pleasure of Rumination:* Walking the dog is much more than a daily chore. It's a release, an escape, an interlude for contemplation of life's mysteries, such as: Why does George pee the way he does? Some dogs squat, some tilt, some just stand there and let 'er rip. George daintily lifts one rear leg, rotates his hips, and stretches his neck out, as if disassociating himself from his nether regions. It's the mind-body dichotomy personified, graceful as Oksana Baiul doing one of those slow, one-legged turns to something by Tchaikovsky. After he finishes, he performs his moonwalk, taking little backward steps with his front paws while clawing the ground with his back legs. Then he repositions himself by the same spot, but this time facing the other way. Then up goes the leg and the back arches and the neck bends back, and it's Oksana time again. He doesn't do this just once, you understand. A single whiz involves as many as six or eight stops, George leaving souvenirs where'er we roam.

George's bladder can't be much bigger than a radish. How he manages to dole out his precious bodily fluids in such tiny increments surpasseth all understanding. And to what end? Is he asserting his dominance, presumably over the dogs whose pee marks he's peeing on, like overwriting a disk? I know the experts say George is simply marking his territory. This means that George believes his domain includes most of Prospect Park, the vestibule of a local Japanese restaurant, and great swaths of upstate New York. He would've claimed Saks Fifth Avenue, too, but the security guard blocked the door. Why would George want to mark Women's Better Dresses for his turf?

I think the reason much of George's marking behavior doesn't make much sense to me is that it doesn't make sense, period. In *The Truth about Dogs*, Stephen Budiansky notes that dogs have an instinct to keep their living areas clean, but not a living area the size of an apartment or house. For an area that big, the instinct is to mark with urine and scat, which is the scientific term for poo. This is a puzzlement faced by everybody who has ever had to house-train a dog.

My favorite walk of the day is the morning one, because that's when I take George up to Prospect Park for off-leash time. Prospect Park is the one Olmsted and Vaux designed *after* Central Park, when they really knew what they were doing. Widely regarded as a masterpiece, it has another distinction, as well: Prospect Park is the dog-friendliest city park in the United States.

THE PEACEABLE KINGDOM

*A sense of enlarged freedom is to
all, at all times, the most certain
and the most valuable gratification
afforded by a park.*

— Frederick Law Olmsted, preliminary
plan for Prospect Park, 1866

It's difficult to explain why being licked to consciousness by a dog with morning mouth is better than it sounds. As a means of waking up, it is effective, which is more than I can say for many clock radios, alarms, telephones, people, garbage trucks, and jackhammers I have known. There's no rolling over and going back to sleep after George's ministrations, because by then he's annexed all the blankets.

I'm not saying it's my preferred way to get up, you understand. I like to arise gradually, very gradually, to the sound of dulcet voices speaking reasonably on NPR. But the George method has a unique property. It makes me laugh. George's wake-up calls make everyone in the family laugh. And laughing in the morning is, historically, just not like us. Five days out of seven, one of us has to go to school, the other two to work. Besides, don't you read the papers? What is there to laugh about? So, while we're all grateful for the morning giggles George provides from time to time, we're glad it's not a daily occurrence, and we're also glad the morning mouth smell rinses right off.

"You're not going up to the park this morning, I shouldn't think," my wife says. I am briefly puzzled, then stung, then the wet hum outside the window reminds me that it was pouring last night when we went to bed; it's pouring now. It doesn't matter.

That's life on the Dawn Patrol.

Most mornings it's automatic. Get up, feed George, look at the paper, fume, unload the dishwasher, head out 8 a.m. Initial progress is slow, as George has his sniff'n'pee at all his favorite spots. Sometimes I apply what Tyril the trainer called "the pop," the little yank on the leash that supposedly tells your dog it's time to move. It must be crisply done, pulling the leash down and away, so as to minimize pressure on the windpipe, but, still, it's yanking. The pops move him, but then George comes to his next spot. So I yank him again. He's walking and stopping and I'm yanking and walking and saying, "Come on, George. Let's go, George" with increasing insistence, and every so often my voice is so angry it turns heads, human heads. What am I getting fussed about?

But this is not one of those mornings. Just before we head out, the rain slakes, and some sun appears. George is positively strutting and I almost am, too.

A venerable clumber spaniel, the most perfectly named of all breeds, lumbers cumbersomely toward us. George and the clumber pause for curt but courteous bum-sniffs, then move on. The man attached to the clumber's leash and I nod at each other.

Farther up the block, I see Amy, looking tense. I greet her, pat her on the head, and proffer half a treat. Amy's person and I nod, too. On Prospect Park West, I pass a woman cooing to her old golden retriever as she holds a water bottle to the dog's mouth. Most of the water falls to the ground. "She never learned to lick her lips when she's finished drinking, so she just walks around dripping, don't you, my darling? Come on, Blanche, move those legs. It's doggie aerobics. Feel the burn," she says, urging the loping creature through its morning routine.

Along the way there are more familiar faces and hellos to Sarah, Mel, Charlie, Vince, Wilson, Watson, Bob, Rock, Miles, Gizmo, Gadget, Gidget, Stella, Rusty, Lamby, and Jack. The human faces are familiar, too, but not so vividly and I have no names to put with them.

I read an article that interpreted the trend of giving dogs human names as a sublimation of child-rearing instinct into pet love. "Dogs are the new children" was the thrust of the argument, as if by naming a dog Ed we're upsetting the natural order of things, in which dogs are all called Spot and Rover.

Actually, it's more accurate to say that children are the new dogs. Properly bred and groomed children confer status on parents the way pedigreed dogs once did. Besides, the line between a dog name and a nondog name is thin and getting thinner all the time, though I admit I've never met anyone named Fido. But what about Rusty or Chip? And where do the name police stand on names that aren't names at all, like Turbo, Radio, or Stereo, all Brooklyn dogs of good standing?

Any dog person knows that a dog's name is just the beginning, the baseline for a lifetime of endless variations, many based on simple, not to say idiotic, repetitions and distortions that riff on terms of endearment and/or derision. Many of these names are never used outside the home. Many are used only when alone with the dog. Embarrassing nicknames pose a threat to dog people that cat people do not face, which is using one in public. Here, in an act of courage that my family is not going to like, I reveal all our nicknames for George to date:

The George

Mr. George
George
Georgie Boy
Boy George
Jorge
Georg
Georgejito
Georges
Yurgis
Yorick
Cutey
Cuteness
Cutius Maximus
Little Boy
Little Boy-boy
Little Boy-boy-boy
Little Doggie Boy

Leetle Boyoyoyo
Little Doggie Jesus
Little Doggie Buddha
Little Doggie Doggie
Stinky
Smell Dog
Death Breath
Baby George
Babyness
Señor Babyness
Babycakes
Pootie
Poo-ta-ta
Poopie-head
Gorgeous George
Wee Geordie
Snoop Money G.

More important than its function as inspiration for verbal improvisation, dog naming is also an act of cultural preservation. Are there any people named Edith or Mildred anymore? I know a couple of dachshunds who are, not to mention Vera the great Dane, Desiree the sheepdog, Lola the Newfie, and Rufus and Nigel the I-know-not-whats. For some reason, poodle people seem to favor high-falutin' monikers like Raphael and Atticus. And I am sure that somewhere, right now, there are dogs named Murgatroyd, Ethelred, Lydia, Aloysius, names that would be lost to history if dogs didn't answer to them. The Dog World is a living archive of forgotten names.

Max, a little beaglish dog, comes careening across the street and almost collides with George in his zeal to connect. Georgie and he sniff each other calmly, for which I am grateful. Sometimes Max gets up George's nose and there is snapping and barking. They're just squabbles of the moment, but if George repeatedly barks, avoids, or lunges at a particular dog, I take it as a sort of judgment. Take the Welsh terrier around here that George just can't abide, for instance. They snarl and bark and lunge at each other every time they pass by. We, the dogs' people, share practically the identical dialogue we shared the last time it happened. There's never been any serious harm done and it's all very courteous and everything, but the truth is it's the other damn dog's problem.

I suppose this means I somehow think George is a judge of character, which I know can't be right. If you should happen to have a biscuit in your hand, you could be Mengele and George wouldn't care.

Food provides a clarity of purpose that obliterates other considerations.

Maxie's person and I chat about little dogs with aggression on their minds. It's clearly on her mind as she tells me how worried she was when Maxie took off running with Lucky and Arrow, two big rottweiler-shepherd mixes who play so bumptiously that it's hard to tell they're not fighting. I make reassurances and move on. I know the names of every dog I've passed; the people with the dogs, a paltry few. It is in this tradition that no superfluous last names were obtained for this book. I didn't think it polite to ask.

George picks up the pace as we traverse the little high-walled path that cuts through the park's surrounding berm and provides the first layer of insulation from city hubbub. We pass the little baby playground where a group of young men are practicing t'ai chi while the babies are still asleep at home, across the roadway and down an incline to the edge of the Long Meadow, ninety acres of grassy sward stretching for over a mile between the park's inner roadway and the densely wooded Ravine. It is believed to be the largest open space in any city park in the country, six times the size of the Sheep

Meadow in Central Park, and not once the site of a Simon and Garfunkel reunion. Virtually every undulation in the earth and every copse of trees has been placed there by design. "People think there was this beautiful spot, so they put a wall around it," says Tupper Thomas, head of the Prospect Park Conservancy. "But this place was built to look this way. It's Disneyland." To me it looks like nature, but better.

Ursula the French bulldog runs up and leans into my shins. Her sinus procedure seems to have healed nicely. So has the bladder infection that's been bothering Daisy, the gentle red Doberman who always tries to get George to chase her. The other regular morning Frenchie, Jean-Claude, is a star of the meadow, recognized and greeted by one and all. This morning he is wheezing hard as ever, but to no apparent ill effect. Perhaps this is because his head is so big in proportion to his little body that he can suck in sufficient air. (He has been described as a cross between a dog and a bowling ball.) He tears around at top speed, bumping amiably into every dog in his path.

Olive the sheepdog comes by for a pat. Joey the whatever is waiting for his well-chewed ball to be kicked, so he can bring it back, so it can be kicked again. Augie the pug is holding his yellow ball in his mouth. If he knows you, he might come over to play catch. He pops the ball out his mouth, making exactly the same sound Leslie Caron makes in "The Night They Invented Champagne" in *Gigi*. You catch the ball and flip it back to Augie. Then he bounces it off his face back to you, or sometimes just off down the rolling veldt of the Long Meadow. The man with the pair of pulis toots short blasts on a whistle. The dogs are definitely moving, but it's hard to say if they're responding to the whistle. The sheltie is there for his daily game of catch with the soft Frisbee, and so is the Nairobi Trio, another regular's three incredibly motley-looking mixes, Homer, Lucy, and Sara. The beautiful great Danes, one black and one silver, stretch and loll, looking more like livestock than pets. I escort George onto the meadow, take a piece of biscuit out of my pocket, tell him to sit, and, as he's chomping his treat, unhook his leash. The joint is jumping, and barking and running and fetching and sniffing, too, because from 9 p.m. to 9 a.m. dogs are allowed on the Long Meadow, and on another area called the Nethermead, without leashes.

Clusters of people hold coffee cups and talk. "I'm feeling a little nauseous this morning. I just started a new antidepressant and my stomach does not like it."

"Drop the chicken bone, Randy. I mean it."

"Siberian huskies are so mellow. He must have been a Buddhist monk in his former life."

One guy, to my never-ending amazement, seems to read the *Times* while bicycling after his Irish setter. Most are strolling singly or in pairs, individual particles with smaller particles, their dogs, circling them in loose orbits. The people are issuing commands with their Darth Vader alpha voices, or they're offering praise and treats with their Kindly Mom voices. I'm alternating between the two, so I sound like a novelty act, Señor Wences and Little Willy. I wonder if the real reason George finds it so easy to ignore either voice is that he's pretending not to know me, the way my wife does when I wear my beret into Manhattan. There's always a dog or two in the deep mud flat that turns into a pond after it rains. Today a beautiful samoyed with fur as white as the inside of an Eskimo Pie saunters nonchalantly into the middle of the enormous puddle and sits deliberately, as the stunned owner musters a choked, beseeching "No? . . ." A persistent voice calling "Zoe! Zoe!" sounds in the distance. Many, perhaps most, of the strollers are wearing big, dopey smiles, nodding and exchanging pleasantries about the weather as if we're all a-headin' off to the clambake in *Carousel*. I am one of the dopey smilers. It is just so not me, historically.

IN SEARCH OF HISTORIC WALKIES

He saw a young woman walking along the promenade; she was fair, not very tall, and wore a toque; behind her trotted a white pomeranian.

— Anton Chekhov, *Lady with a Lapdog*

Dog walking is a recent development. By dog walking, I mean a person and a dog walking together, usually but not necessarily connected by a leash, for the conjoined purposes of exercise, elimination, and society. The activity hardly existed as such before the middle of the twentieth century. The closest we get to it before then is the English sport of beagling, which is like riding to hounds, except without horses. A fox is released and the beagles take off after it. Then a lot of men in tweed jackets take off after the dogs and are immediately left in the dust. My wife's uncle Alfred was a beagler. She tells me beagling is largely an excuse for a pleasant walk with many pub stops along the way. It sounds great, but not feasible on a regular basis in Brooklyn. We just walk.

When you walk your dog, you are tacitly acknowledging that your dog doesn't have enough to do. Walking is a substitute for hunting or tracking or herding or whatever it is that your dog would be doing if it were a working dog. It is also a demonstration, for better or worse, of your affection for, and commitment to, your pet.

Dog walking is mostly an urban phenomenon, but it's also the quotidian act of quality time between pet and person and the principal form of exercise for most owned dogs. Dogs in this country tend to be pets, not working animals, and most pet owners don't have the inclination or time or skill to train their dogs for agility trials or lure coursing or the show ring. But just about every dog, city or country or in between, gets walked on a leash from time to time.

It wasn't always this way. There are plenty of dogs, but no dogs walked, in the *Canterbury Tales*, the plays of Shakespeare, *War and Peace*, or *Dombey and Son*. The prophet Tobias walks along with his little dog in the Apocrypha, but since the dog has some connection to the angel also accompanying them, I don't think it counts as an example of dog walking. Chekhov's *Lady with a Lapdog* never walks it, even though it seems to me the barky little thing needs one. The 1902 Sears Catalogue offers an array of dog chains, whips, and cleaning items, but no leashes. The word "lead," which the British use when they mean "leash," was not used in that way until 1896, according to the *O.E.D.* (The word "leash," on the other hand, dates to the writings of St. Gregory in the thirteenth century, though only as a restraint for hunting dogs. But you knew that.)

If the earliest dog walkers are lost in the mists, the earliest dog-walking regulations are not. In the eleventh century, the Forest Laws of King Canute required the king's tax collectors to remove the middle toes of mastiffs to prevent them from chasing the royal deer in the royal forests. Granted, this isn't exactly a leash law, but it does address the same issue leash laws do: keeping dogs in line.

Since pretty much all the forests and therefore all the deer were royal, eleventh-century Britain was a tough time to be a mastiff, even though such big, impressive dogs probably were living well as the property of landed gentry. Back then, most dogs belonged to the aristocracy or to nobody. Noblemen in the time of Charlemagne brought their hunting hounds right into church, presumably to get an early start after services wrapped up. The absence of antique laws governing dogs is directly related to the fact that rich people don't like being told what to do, or even what their dogs should do.

Even into the nineteenth century, the first time there was a large middle class that could afford pets and the popularity of dogs spread down the social food chain, there were few laws governing their treatment or behavior, at least outside of parks and cemeteries. New York City didn't have a leash law until 1942, when it replaced a law requiring muzzles.

I was amazed to learn this, and pictured the clotted streets of today's downtown teeming with unleashed dogs wearing muzzles. I didn't like the image one bit, though it's easy to forget that urban manners mean different things at different times. Leash laws mean less in an environment where many dogs are not owned, and in 1928 there were 85,000 stray dogs on the streets of New York. That's about four times as many as there are today.

Animal law prior to the late twentieth century had everything to do with preventing disease and injury and very little to do with being nice to pets. In 1860, for instance, New York had no leash law, but it did have one forbidding free-ranging pigs below 86th Street in Manhattan. Having grown up on 85th Street a scant century later, I salute those long-gone lawmakers for their perspicacity and a job well done.

New York streets have never been as safe for dogs as those of smaller towns, of course. In upstate Ithaca, New York, dogs have been allowed to wander the grounds, hallways, and even classrooms of Cornell University since at least as far back as the 1920s. Decades of hearsay held that a large bequest was contingent upon the dogs' free run of the campus. No such bequest actually exists, but these dogs thrived, pariahs who became wards of the community. Some became legendary. In the 1930s, a bulldog named Napoleon regularly rode a streetcar down the hill into town, loitered around the bars, and caught the last car back to campus. A three-legged husky named Tripod cadged food outside the student union in the 1960s, and an Irish setter named Mike audited drama classes, always rising to stretch just before the bell rang.

Those days are gone. Cornell now prohibits off-leash dogs on campus, which seems unduly harsh considering all the money Cornell has made from dogs. The most profitable of the more than 300 patents Cornell holds is the one for canine parvovirus vaccine. A little special treatment doesn't seem inappropriate.

SLIPPING THE LEASH

No quadrupeds except placed in the Park by the Commissioners, and except dogs when controlled by a line of suitable strength not more than six feet in length, . . . shall be driven or conducted into the Park or allowed to remain in it.

— Frederick Law Olmsted,
Ordinances Applicable to the Ordinary
Use of the Central Park, 1873

Veterinarian Thomas Parker grew up a block away from Prospect Park in the 1970s and walked the family dogs there. "You took them up to the edge of the park, took off their leashes, and let 'em go."

When I mentioned this to Tupper Thomas, who came to the Prospect Park Conservancy in 1980, her retort was sharp. "In the seventies, he was probably the only person in the park, so who was going to give him a ticket?"

Others remember plenty of people around to give tickets. In those days, New York was in dire financial straits and there was a sense that crime and general street nastiness were on the rise. Quality-of-life issues were in the news. In Prospect Park, a force of ninety-odd Park Rangers was urged to enforce the laws on the books.

Attempts to clamp down on wayward dog owners were met with howling objections. My friend Jerome Vitucci recalls park police showing up to ticket the half-dozen or so dog people who'd brought their pets up to the park at seven o'clock on Thanksgiving morning. Jerome is one of those who lobbied hard for off-leash hours in Prospect Park, if lobbying is the word. He recalls a particular walk in Prospect Park in the late 1970s. "It was nine or so in the morning and I was coming out of the park with Mikey the junkyard shepherd and Mr. Bones the pit bull. We were close to the park entrance so I was putting their leashes on. This park ranger or cop or whatever he was pulls up behind me in his cruiser and gets out and he's wearing jodhpurs, like a Nazi," Jerome recalls. "He told me I didn't have my dogs on leash and I said I knew and I was putting them on. He said he needed to see some ID. I told him I didn't have anything, I'd just walked out the door without a wallet or anything, but if he wanted to he could follow me home and I'd show him my ID. And I started off. The guy jumped on me, so I knelt down to keep the dogs from lunging at the cop, and that flipped him over my head, and the next thing I knew he was calling backup and I was in jail."

The Prospect Park Rangers are cut from different cloth nowadays, if the two who ticketed me in 2003 for violating Olmsted's rule are any indication.

Let me say right up front that I was in violation of the law and that ignorance of the law is no excuse, even though it was the very first time I'd let George go without the trainer in attendance. I wasn't holding George's thirty-foot-long training leash even though I could have stepped on it at any time, stopping George in his tracks, and I was much less than six feet away from him, so the leash was in the spirit of the law even if not the letter. It's still no excuse.

I might have talked my way out of it if it hadn't been for the other dog walker nearby when the park rangers' SUV appeared. One got out and informed us our dogs were not under our control. Stealthily slipping a foot over the leash, I apologized humbly, eyes downcast, a strategy that has gotten me out of a speeding ticket or two, so I was hopeful. But the other dog walker took offense at the Ranger's words.

"My dog most certainly is under my control," she said curtly. The rangers pointed out that dogs could not be off-leash on the Long Meadow in midafternoon. I tried everything from telepathy to semaphore to get my fellow miscreant to shut up, but she just got more and more insistent that her dog was as responsive to her as if she were on a leash. By this point, both rangers were placidly writing summonses for each of us, which got the dogger even madder. Finally, when the ranger who'd been filling out her summons handed it over, she hissed, "Dog hater!"

I started to say something about never having seen this woman before in my life. One of the rangers said wearily, "Ma'am, I'm not a dog hater, I'm a dog lover. You just can't have your dog off-leash."

As their SUV and I both eased away, I could hear the woman still indignantly standing her ground, making her case. "I find it very hard to believe that you love dogs . . ."

(On July 14, 2004, I finally received a judgment of guilty and the maximum fine of a hundred bucks. Still, I'd hung on to my hundred bucks for over a year, and one should be grateful for small victories.)

Prospect Park was a gritty and desolate place in the 1970s. The baseball diamonds and athletic fields got regular use from surrounding schools and local leagues, but by 1980, visits to the park had fallen to 1.7 million a year. Tupper Thomas initiated off-leash hours (from 9 a.m. to 9 p.m. on the Long Meadow only) in the early 1980s as a way to get more people into the park, especially at an hour when it wasn't being used much at all. And it was an immediate success. As dog people took to the meadow, runners began to appear on the roadways. Cyclists followed, then birders and barbecuers. Crime statistics went down. Visits went up. The park got safer.

By 1996, there was trouble in paradise. Dogs were off-leash in the park at all hours and all over the place, bugging picnickers and disrupting soccer games. Tupper called a meeting of dog owners to remind them that the park's off-leash hours were a privilege, not a right, and subject to retraction, if restrictions on where and when dogs can cavort were not enforced. "I remember a very angry owner and her collie whining in unison," she recalls. "But out of that meeting came FIDO Brooklyn." FIDO is the Fellowship in the Interest of Dogs and their Owners. FIDO raises money, makes sure its members toe the off-leash line, works with the park conservancy to resolve conflicts with the birders and ball players, and sponsors events like Bark the Herald Angels Sing (caroling dogs and people on the Long Meadow) and the annual Spring Pupnic. (Dogs! Puns! Why, lord, why?) FIDO led the campaigns for dog-height water fountains and the park's justly famous Dog Beach, where dogs can swim without damaging the vegetation in the recently restored Upper Pool.

Central Park and other New York parks now have off-leash hours, and parks in other cities have adopted them, too, but

Prospect Park remains the seedbed of off-leash liberty. Prospect Park visits are up to 7 million a year. Allowing for sick days, impossible weather, deadlines, and travel, I figure that George and I account for close to 300 of 'em.

HIGHLY SUCCESSFUL WALKS AND THE PEOPLE WHO TAKE THEIR DOGS FOR THEM

"If you don't know how to do it, I'll show you how to walk the dog."

— Rufus Thomas, "Walkin' the Dog"

It's a brisk but not crushingly cold Sunday morning. George and I turn into the park's Garfield Street entrance behind a woman in navy leggings and an indeterminately drab sweatshirt cinched with a lime green fanny pack that holds the CD player whose headphones perch atop her tight salt-and-pepper curls. Springing along on a long leash tied to the woman's waist is a miniature poodle with a red ball in its mouth. The two reach the park's inner roadway. Wise walkers pause at the curb by the traffic light even on week-

125

ends, when the road is closed to automobiles, because there are often park vehicles, bike riders, skaters, and other random traffic on the road. The leggings lady takes a cursory glance, sees no cars, and power-walks ahead, oblivious to the speeding cyclist who has materialized in the bike lane from around the bend. He's wearing one of those gaudy, skintight outfits and a helmet and he's moving at a terrific clip. The woman, lost in her music, doesn't break stride.

"Look out, look out, look out!" the cyclist cries, then: "GOD-DAMN IT, WATCH WHERE YOU'RE GOING!" as he brakes rapidly, fishtailing as he slows before the poodle and the woman who, without missing a beat, or even turning her head, delivers a curt, tightly enunciated "F— you, a—hole!"

An ugly pause hangs in the air and then we all go on our way. I recognize the voice from parents association meetings at my son's school. The woman's nickname among some of us is "Angry Mom."

There is a lesson to be learned here, and it is this: You can coast through most of life on obliviousness, hostility, and a foul mouth, but proper dog walking demands something better. The following is a provisional list of requirements. There may be more:

1. Dog names only, please: When your dog encounters another and they fall to butt-sniffing, it is polite to ask the other dog's name. Asking the other human's name, however, is the social equivalent of sniffing that person's butt, and on the first date, too. It is Just Not Done. This can go on for years and has a kind of ripple effect, so that if you should run into the person without the dog and you both recognize each other, your greeting is usually restricted to a polite nod, because what are you going to say? "Hello, Dexter's person!" Not everybody can do that.

2. Get over your craving for recognition: Nothing personal, but it is unlikely that anybody you meet through your dog will recognize you when you are canine-free. Dog people tend to know one another only by their dogs. Don't be hurt. After George arrived, my family got chatty with a man across the street who has a black Lab and always carries a pocketful of cookies. As you'd expect, George gazes wistfully up at his door whenever we pass his house. One day the man asked us if we'd just moved to the block. It was George who'd just moved in; we'd been here for thirteen years.

3. Work on your leash skills: You'll be

glad you did. Among the health benefits of regular dog walking is the heightened co-ordination and sense of balance that come from moving in a more or less straight line while your dog is not. For me this involves turning in circles while still moving for-ward to avoid superfluous passing of the leash from hand to hand. Sometimes it's just easier to swivel, but not too fast or you'll get dizzy. I could train George to walk on one side or the other, I suppose, but I'll be damned if I'll interfere with my dog's right to choose.

4. Eschew the Flex-leash, WMD (weapon of manual destruction): Olmsted's leash directive for Central Park predates the Parks Department regulations and any other leash law for the rest of New York. The parks have changed since he wrote it. Central Park's Sheep Meadow ac-tually had sheep on it, also a shepherd. So did the Long Meadow in Brooklyn. The sheep left in the 1930s, banished by Robert Moses, but the law on the books today is essentially Olmsted's, and is yet another example of the man's farsighted vision, for by limiting leash length to six feet, he made the Flex-leash illegal. Flex-leashes are long nylon lines that unspool or retract from a plastic housing. They are ostensibly a means of giving your dog a little extra room to move while you maintain control. What usually happens is that you forget if too much line has played out or too little, or if you've locked the catch or not. Then your dog takes off in fierce pursuit of a squirrel or Popsicle wrapper. Depending on your dog's weight and velocity, you will be jerked off balance and drop your cappuccino. That's if the catch is locked. If it's not locked, it becomes entwined around trees, bushes, other dogs' leashes, other dog walkers' legs as well as your own, causing you to be knocked off balance and drop your cappuccino. Look closely at the plastic housing and you'll see little bas-relief illustrations warning users not to wind the Flex-leash around fingers or forearms on pain of amputation. If you retract one too fast, you could lose an eye. The Flex-leash is an unsatisfactory compromise between a leash and no leash, Olmsted and I agree.

5. Watch your mouth: Be very careful of what you say about anyone else's dog. If you have nothing nice to say, shut up or lie. And don't mess around with ambiguities, either. I once remarked perfectly innocently that a dog looked comical. "What's that supposed to mean?" the dog's owner asked unsmilingly. Occasionally, Long Meadow neophytes refer to George as "the other George," because there is another Norfolk named George in Prospect Park. I set such people straight, and pronto. That other Norfolk is "the other George." You got a problem with that?

6. *Dress for the weather:* You are not passing through, you are actually in it. Besides, what's the point of owning a lot of hideous, technically advanced clothing if you're not going to wear it?

7. *Conceal your bags:* You already know this, but a reminder can't hurt.

8. *Don't be too damn cute.* I'm a man of gentle demeanor, and the only time I have ever felt I understood where someone like Hannibal Lecter is coming from was listening to a young couple pushing a stroller and gushing over George and their King Charles spaniel puppy. The wife had a piping voice like Glinda the Good and she talked fast: "Oh, yes, aren't you a cutie, are you a cute little boy? Are you? Yes! What a cutie, cutie, cutie pie. Is you a cutie? Yes, you is!" And the guy said more or less the same, but in the sort of dull, affectless voice I associate with religious cults. I thought their sugary tones were fine for their baby and fine for their doggywoggy, too. But I was happy to see George regarding them with his skeptical face, one luxuriant eyebrow raised inquisitively. A dog of discernment is not so easily won.

THE PROFESSIONALS

Do you need a responsible person to take care of your pet while you are not at home? I can stay with your dog overnight at your house or he can stay with me at my apartment. I can feed and hang out with your cat too.

— Brooklyn dog walker's circular, c. 2002

One of the delights of an exhibit called Petropolis at the New York Historical Society in 2003 was *The Incredible Dog Walker,* a wonderfully antic sculpture of seventeen dogs being walked by one woman. The dogs are of many different sizes and shapes, and the walker seems completely unfazed. The sculptor who created it, John Costanza, said he was inspired by a real woman he saw walking that many dogs on Madison Avenue.

131

There's a local walker here who sometimes walks six or eight dogs at a time, all big ones. I see him on the street, leashes in one hand, cell phone in the other. I've seen him in the park during off-leash hours with as many as ten dogs between him and his partner. Once a fellow nonpro and I exchanged smiles as the bunch of them went by and then said softly, "That's too many dogs." A couple of years ago this walker was making his rounds and had tied several dogs to a house gate while returning or collecting another dog. A car drove by and one of the dogs, a ridgeback, lunged at it. The ridgie's collar snapped and the poor creature was run over. The dog belonged to the family of a 9/11 victim, hideously enough.

You would think that an incident like that would cut into a dog walker's business, but not for this particular fellow. There was widespread debate wherever doggers gathered, and the general feeling was that the collar's snapping off was an accident. That the dogs were tied to a gate is troubling, but it's hard to devise an alternative, aside from ushering all the dogs up and down every stoop. The fellow is still very much in business. The local Dog World looked at the guy and the obvious connection he had with the dogs and decided he was still one of its citizens, a conclusion I agree with, though not to the extent of ever letting him walk George.

Dog walkers have been a fixture of the urban landscape since the 1980s, when the model nuclear family suddenly seemed to grow two careers and children with fully booked schedules. Professional dog walking is associated with actors, artists, and other marginal types. An article in *New York* magazine in 2003 portrayed them as mostly freaks and weirdos whose reasons for doing the work rarely had anything to do with any fondness for dogs. One owner in the piece came upon her dachshund and the walker she'd hired in Washington Square Park. They were dressed in matching Mexican outfits, with sombreros and ponchos, and the walker was panhandling. Another came home to find her walker, a man this time, dancing around the apartment in the owner's new dress. Yet another was videotaped coming into an apartment, taking the money left for the walk, and leaving without taking the dog out at all.

They're great stories and I don't doubt them, but these walkers are nothing like the walkers I know. In fact, they are not like any dog walkers I've ever heard of. Which is not to say that dog walkers aren't a strange breed, because they are. But what's odd about them is not the lengths to which they'll go to abuse their trust, but the fact that most of them would rather be with dogs than people. Dog walkers spend a lot of time with dogs, and every one I've asked prefers things that way. For many, dog walking is a way to simplify life, to escape from pressure, to regroup. For one I spoke to, it is a haven after a personal meltdown involving the unexpected deaths of two close friends. Some walkers will go to great lengths to avoid human interaction. One Manhattan couple I spoke to returns home each evening to a detailed handwritten note from their walker, with a full report on food and elimination and a general summary of the dog's mood through the day. The couple leaves notes about schedule changes and other arrangements. In seven years they have seen their walker four times.

Unsurprisingly, dog walking is an unregulated industry. There is something called the National Association of Professional Dog Walkers, but its Web site as of this writing lists one walker in Brooklyn and two in Manhattan, one of whom will walk dogs only twelve pounds or under.

Anyone can set up a dog-walking business. Those who do enter the small world of workers who have so intimate a view of you and your foibles that the normal employer's comfort zone is compromised. Dog walkers have the ability, like babysitters and contractors, to make you feel guilty or stupid, sometimes both.

Around here, I've been able to size up the local walkers in situ. There's the slender, cheerful person with short graying hair I've seen walking dogs ever since we moved here in 1989, who seems to know and be known by everyone, and of whose gender I have never been sure. There's the chipper young thing with a voice so sugary it hurts my ears, but Georgie adores her. Every time we see her he goes all winsome, waggling his butt and leaping up to lick her face. The dour but extremely gossipy older woman walker told me the chirpy, outgoing one is really a conniver who was stealing her business, but I've learned since to take the gossipy lady's opinions with a pound or two of salt. She and I have one enduring conversational topic, the difference between Norfolks and Norwiches, which she can never keep straight and which I'm always ready to go over one more time. It is to sigh.

Dog walkers have singular ideas of what they want to do. There's a gray-haired lady who specializes in short spins around the neighborhood with little dogs, and the wiry young Icelandic guy who tends to big dogs that need serious exercise. When some friends moved nine blocks recently, their longtime dog walker declared them out of his zone and dropped them.

Can you imagine a baby-sitter or cleaning person dumping a regular gig over nine blocks? I can't. But reliable dog walkers are in demand. When I asked the chipper, sugary-voiced one if she had a card, she told me her schedule was too full to consider any new clients.

My search ended there. I decided that hiring a walker would be the coward's way out. Part of the deal when we got George from Kay was that the dog would have company. That's me. Anyway, what were we talking about? According to all the guides, Norfolks need half an hour of exercise a day, in the form of walk or play. Figure a longish walk and two or three shorter walks. I walk that much in the course of a day anyway. So what's the big deal?

This was before I learned to view dog

guides skeptically. Half an hour? Maybe if you're chasing him up and down stairs. Otherwise, George needs two to three times that much exercise or he's bouncing off the walls. And so I walked George with a vengeance. In those early months, I'd put George in a spiffy blue harness, hook on the scary Flex-leash, and set forth. Together, George and I have walked every path in Prospect Park. We've found the remnant of a derelict bamboo grove near the Vale of Kashmir. George has sprinkled his blessing on the fence that protects the Camperdown Elm. We've climbed to the top of Lookout Point, walked alongside the Lullwater, and traversed a substantial length of the fence that surrounds the Quaker cemetery wherein Montgomery Clift is buried.

With exercise like that, you'd assume the little beast would spend the rest of the day asleep or amusing himself with his toys or just basking in the warm, alpha glow of my company. Not so. My company isn't necessarily enough for him, and he has his ways of letting me know. For a while, I crated him for a few hours a day. Everybody knows all dogs love to be crated.

Outside the Dog World, a crate is a big box, often made of wood, that holds pianos or eggs. But here, a crate is a portable cage. George's is a gray-beige plastic with big slits. It's big enough for George to stand in and turn around, but not much bigger. Crates are highly recommended for house-training puppies. Thereafter they're used for naps, relaxing, and sometimes, confusingly, as a place of exile and punishment. Generally, it's said, dogs like hanging out in their crates because it reminds them of the caves they lived in back when they were wolves. Ours was a useful, if hideous, addition to our living room decor until it was time for bed, when I got to schlep the thing upstairs to my son's bedroom, a task that had no impact whatsoever on my lower back issues. It's a fact, many dogs love their crates; I'm not denying it.

However. How-goddamn-ever. To me, crating a dog is like putting it into lockdown and I found the whole business depressing, especially when George would just stare at me through the slits in his accusatory way. So I was pleased when he began to sleep outside his crate. Now he reposes on any of a number of favored spots, currently a fragrant pile of old towels next to my night table. When he gets nostalgic for the caves of his atavistic, wolfen unconscious, he lurks under a chair.

The crate is in the basement.

As we've all gotten to know each other, it has become clear that George needs society as much as he needs exercise. He is a gregarious soul, if one can be gregarious without being able to talk. A life of whiling away the hours near a guy stuck in a chair, no matter how generously interlarded with walkies and treats, is no life for him. Intuitive as I'm sure George is, I don't think he has any idea that I am not happy to be the guy stuck in the chair. I would much prefer to hang with George than work. He doesn't get that. I think my behavior pisses him off when he thinks about it, which is usually not long after napping. Then he stares at me plaintively, like a kid in a UNICEF ad, and that makes me feel guilty at first and then disproportionately angry, so it's a good thing for all concerned that I finally met Eva.

Eva came to New York from Sweden to work on Wall Street but didn't like it. She left banking to become a veterinary technician at a clinic in Park Slope. When I first heard of her, from the owner of Macy the Tibetan terrier, she was taking groups of dogs to Prospect Park or to a nearby dog run. If the weather was foul, the dogs romped in her apartment. Although she had encountered George, she came over to meet him formally before he could join the group. Such a meeting is necessary so that Eva can look for signs of aggression. She also listens to the people's language for code, like "he gets excited when he sees other dogs." Organizing a group of dogs to play together is not the same as walking them. Eva and her people walk several unneutered dogs, but she will not allow an unneutered male into the playgroups. George demonstrated his sit and his down and sniffed her hand speculatively. I felt the way I did during my son's interviews for pre-K: eager to please but obscurely indignant.

Georgie took to the whole playgroup concept like a duck toller to water. On appointed days, he lunges down the stoop to greet his pals with abundant butt-sniffing and nuzzling, and they're off. If my son's around when he gets home, there's strutting and barking and jumping up on the sofa in his delightful way. If not, he sips a little water and pokes around, waits to see if I'll come across with half a biscuit (time well spent, since I'm usually good for it). Then he'll poke at a toy and look through me as if I'm not even there.

Fortunately, I'm too big for pettiness.

George doesn't have to be paying a lot of attention to me, much less doing the whole fawning bit, to be infinitely diverting. I like to watch the subtle gradations in his responses to the different members of Eva's growing staff who come to pick him up in the morning. Most of them are immigrants and no two of them have the same accent, and George's behavior is slightly different with each. If it's Eva, he goes ape, whinnying and leaping up to turn the doorknob himself. Same for Beate, who's from Poland. If it's Ava, Enya, or Gosha, he paws the ground to get me to open the door faster so he can meet and greet the day's canine klatch. Who's there today, Truffle or Moxie or Miles or Ruby or Edith or Rockie or Rudy or Macy or . . . ?

You could write a book about George, really, and the opportunity to do that is what, ironically, has put the kibosh on our quality time, temporarily at least. I have had to choose between the morning walk or an unencumbered day. If George and I have our morning constitutional together, we get off to a great start, but by midafternoon we're both getting edgy.

So I took steps. Better he have broadening experiences with other dogs, I decided unselfishly. In addition to the rotating rep of locals, there is the ever-changing ensemble of Eva's own dogs. They are rescues, strays, or dogs who belonged to clients who have moved away or couldn't handle the responsibility. Beate inherited her dog, a long-haired miniature dachshund named Mildred who had triggered a violent allergy in her owner. *Et tu,* Mildred?

Fortunately, I still have the later walks, but they aren't nearly as much fun as that off-leash hour in the morning, which has a special frisson because I never thought George would be able to do it. Shortly after he arrived, I shared the story of our Christmas surprise with an out-of-town friend who, unbeknownst to me, turned out to be very familiar with Norfolk terriers. She confirmed all our hopes: delightful dogs, friendly, playful, etc. But she also said, "Don't even think about obedience classes. And don't even *think* about taking him off the leash. He'll chase a squirrel or something and you'll never get him back."

My friend overestimated the power of George's blood lust. His encounters with squirrels have been brief and inconclusive. They stare at each other like forgetful actors wondering whose line it is. For

George, as for many of the dogs in Prospect Park, the strongest instinct is the garbage drive. On a warm Sunday morning in summer, when the garbage cans that ring the picnic tables are full from Saturday's feasts and ripening in the sun, even obedient dogs ignore their masters' cries and dash off to scarf Ho-Ho wrappers and grease-soaked paper with alacrity.

4. "sit" and other unanswered prayers

SYMPATHY FOR THE ROYAL

"You gonna bark all day, little doggy, or are you gonna bite?"

— Mr. Blonde (Michael Madsen)
in *Reservoir Dogs*

I am not much of a monarchist. My fascination with contemporary royalty pretty much starts and stops with an abiding desire to have a suit made by Prince Charles's tailor. So I was surprised in April 2002 when, during a televised news report about the court appearance of Britain's Princess Anne, the dowdy but dutiful one, to answer for the behavior of her bull terrier, Dotty, I found myself supportively muttering "You go, Your Highness!" at the screen.

Here's what happened: While walking the private grounds of Windsor Castle, Dotty broke away from the princess and her husband, Commodore Tim. The dog bolted across the divider between private and public areas and bit a couple of boys who were on a tour. The princess pleaded guilty. The question to be decided was whether or not Dotty should be put down. The crown prosecutor said Dotty bit the boys; the defense lawyer maintained she only "nipped" them.

Why such solidarity with a royal who, after all, would not know me from a Welsh miner until I opened my mouth? Because, Princess Anne, I feel your pain. I can relate. I know that Dotty only nipped. How do I know this? Because not a week before, George — sweet, winsome George — bit a carpenter as he stood in our vestibule. And that, too, was only a nip.

Fortunately, there was very little blood, and the guy took it completely in stride. I think he understood that when a fellow of his impressive height and virile demeanor shows up at our home wearing a tool belt, then George really has no alternative. We were lucky. If the carpenter hadn't been such a mellow fellow, there could have been real trouble.

The distinction between "bite" and "nip" is crucial and protean. It is a shifting frontier, a delicate balance point between the size of the dog, the size of the bite, and whose beast did the dental deed. It can be the difference between a disagreement and a lawsuit, between a dog with aggression issues and no dog at all. A dog who bites strangers can be removed from its owner. The legal leash is short and extends no further than the dog's immediate human family, who can be bitten with impunity.

Here's the way it works: If my dog did it, it's a nip. If your dog did it, it's a bite. George never bites; he nips, period. Furthermore, he is high-spirited, not aggressive. Like in the summer, when he nips at my son's swim trunks to pull 'em down. High spirits.

Remarkably, this was precisely the line of argument taken by the princess's defense. The crown prosecutor said Dotty "bit" the boys, causing them to be "traumatized." The princess's defending barrister countered that the dog had only "nipped" the boys, causing "boo-boos." Well, he didn't say boo-boos, but he did produce an expert witness to testify that Dotty wasn't vicious, only playful. See the difference?

The princess was permitted to keep her dog on condition that Dotty be on leash in public and muzzled "if necessary." She was required to get training for the dog and pay a fine. Anne got off easy, considering that the last royal to be convicted of a crime before an English court, Charles I, was beheaded in 1649, although he achieved a sort of immortality in the form of the Cavalier King Charles Spaniel.

The families of the injured boys weren't happy, but fines and compensation were paid and life went on, even as things did in my house. George's nip-threatening moments are few and diminishing, so we're able to get away with a certain laxness in our approach. This is because an excitable dog who weighs fifteen pounds is a smaller problem than one who weighs eighty. Do the math.

As George has become better behaved and sporadic lunges less frequent, my view of those moments of aggression has changed. Against my better judgment, which I know I have around here somewhere, I have come to trust George's assessments of unfamiliar people as much as his opinions of unfamiliar dogs. Take the kid who came up our stoop on Halloween in full scary costume and asked to pet George. We agreed and cautioned her to kneel down and slowly extend her hand under his chin, not atop his head, which would scare him and might make him snap at her. The kid nodded, then moved her hand right out over the top of his head, and, sure enough, George went for her. He didn't make contact; my wife and I both flung ourselves on him, even though there really isn't enough of George to accommodate two flung adults. The terrified girl burst into tears anyway. We apologized profusely and plied her with extra Tootsie Rolls, even though the whole thing was her own damn fault.

We were forced to reexamine our views when George bit — that is, nipped — my son's friend Pete, who was twelve at the time, a gentle, personable boy who was by no means wearing a tool belt. I had to face up to the fact that certain people, such as Pete's parents, who are lawyers, might see George's actions in a less forbearing light than I.

In an amazing coincidence, the Pete incident was followed by more trouble for Princess Anne, and of a very similar nature, except worse. Over a year after the attacks on the children, headlines screamed that Dotty had attacked one of the queen's beloved Pembroke Welsh corgis, Pharos, mauling it so badly it had to be put down. Queen Elizabeth's affection for her dogs is well documented, and corgis, with their big broad heads and their stubby little legs, the better to avoid the kicking hooves of the cattle they are bred to herd, inspire quite a bit of affection all on their own. Bull terriers, on the other hand, are an acquired taste. It looked bad for Dotty.

Princess Anne's story and my own begin to diverge at this point. For example, after George bit Pete, the ASPCA did not call for George to be put down, while this is exactly what the RSPCA did vis-à-vis Dotty, declaring her a "rogue dog," who had "bitten once and now has killed." Considering the queen is the charity's patron, these were harsh words, which the RSPCA had to eat a few days later, when a palace spokesman informed a waiting world that Dotty had been falsely accused. The perp was another of Anne's bull terriers, Florence. Less than a week later, Flo bit a royal maid on the leg. There was another flurry of speculation that this dog would be put down, but instead Flo was sentenced to therapy with a psychologist who opined to the papers that she wasn't a dangerous dog, only "feeling a bit cranky on the day." The maid received a personal apology from the queen and negotiations for a settlement got under way. Then, in March 2004, a London man named Clive Mulgrow, described as a "researcher," declared that Dotty, the miscreant who'd bit the kids visiting Windsor, had been particularly loathed by Princess Diana. Mulgrew further suggested that Dot may have hidden in Di and Dodi's car and caused the crash, though he offered no explanation of how the dog might have gotten to Paris.

There is a moral here, and it is that hoity-toity bloodlines are no guarantee of good behavior. The Queen herself sanctioned some dogs behaving badly when Pipkin, Princess Margaret's dachshund, managed to put one of sister Elizabeth's corgis in the family way. The Queen was pleased with the resulting litter and named them dorgies. A portrait of the Queen hangs in the entrance hall of Britain's Kennel Club. The dorgi depicted in that painting is the only likeness of a mixed breed in the whole place.

For those of us without royal pull, teaching your dog to behave is less a matter of noblesse oblige than of real necessity. Fortunately, the Dog World contains masses, vats, metric tons of information on the subject of training, an unending river of books, magazines, theories, Web sites, and many individuals, some qualified and some less so, to explain it all to you. Choice, as we all know, is a good thing, so you would imagine that picking your own preference would be simply a matter of totting up the pros and cons of a particular approach or a particular teacher and picking one.

The reality turns out to be different. The reality is that, in the Dog World, we bring much of the same baggage to pet training as we do to child rearing. Just as the way you raise your children is a response to how you were raised, so is the way you train your dog.

MASTERS AND COMMANDERS

You always know what a dog is thinking. It has four moods. Happy, sad, cross, and concentrating.

— Mark Haddon, *The Curious Incident of the Dog in the Nighttime*

During their retirement, my wife's parents had a mottled gray-black cocker spaniel called Kim. Kim lived outside in a doghouse within a fenced enclosure, but he spent much of his downtime in the living room, sitting on my mother-in-law's feet or by my father-in-law's wing chair. Kim lived to be about eleven or twelve, and even in his later days enjoyed what you would call an active lifestyle: two or three robust daily walks off-lead on the village heath, plus extended patrols of the couple's large, wooded garden.

In the field, apparently, Kim was all you could want in a gun dog, alert and eager and able to retrieve a bird without mangling it in his mouth. He was clearly devoted to both his people, but Kim was fixed above all on the man of the house. When tea was served, which it was about nine times a day, Kim would sit motionless, poised between his master's feet, waiting for his inviolable biscuit. Kim could always tell when it was a pheasant-shooting day because of the way my father-in-law turned on the kitchen light those mornings, and he'd bark and jump exuberantly.

My father-in-law loved him back, always topping up Kim's food bowl with table scraps and regaling us all with tales of

Kim's derring-do, most famously the time he brought down a deer single-handedly. Though he'd never been neutered, Kim was never bred, either, which I thought puzzling, not to say inconsiderate. Why leave the dog intact if you're never going to let him enjoy what you've let him keep? Gonads notwithstanding, Kim was never aggressive with other dogs or people and, according to my father-in-law, "still enjoyed the most *splendid* erections!" When my wife asked "With whom?" he replied smartly, "Himself!" My father-in-law, a retired physician, considered himself a tough-minded man of science, but when Kim got sick and had to be put down, he insisted on doing it himself and, afterward, he wept. In subsequent years, the mere mention of Kim's name would choke him up.

Man and dog were so in tune they were a pleasure to watch together, but less so for my wife than for me. Her father's delight in Kim's subservience bothered her. She felt he'd hoped for much the same eager submission from his children and, surprise surprise, hadn't gotten it. As a parent, she strove to be different from him — not so strict, not so caustic, gentler and more philosophical, more like her mother.

Like my wife's, my parenting style diverges from that of my parents. My father faced life with stoic indifference or passive aggression, depending on your point of view. My mother was angry, frustrated, and vocal. Their terribly unsynchronized responses, quiet desperation (Dad) and noisy desperation (Mom), left my sister and me somewhere on the periphery of their awareness. I've tried to create a quieter, calmer, more consistent, attentive, and upbeat atmosphere than the one in which I grew up. And I've also tried to the very best of my ability not to impose my standards on my son, despite the fact that, when I was his age, I could recite the first eighteen lines of the *The Canterbury Tales* in the original, pre–Great Vowel Shift, Middle English, while my son cannot. In the spirit of fairness, I should add that he excels at shooting the three and Latin, which I never even took.

Despite my friend's warnings about obedience classes, I knew that George was not untrainable. He is, for instance, very well house-trained, with maybe three accidents in the years we've had him. There were a couple of other soiling incidents, but in my view they were not accidents; they were editorials. George was house-trained before we got him by Kay, his breeder. The aspects of George's training that we were responsible for — sitting, staying, that sort of thing — have been a mixed bag success-wise, to be more than charitable. But I knew then as I know now that George's learning difficulties, such as they are, lay with his instructors, not with him.

Before I could train George, I would have to understand his ways, of course. So I turned to the definitive work on the breed, Joan R. Read's *The Norfolk Terrier.* Our dogs, Ms. Read says, are "problem-solvers," imaginative types, not chronic fetchers or herding machines or needy wimps like some breeds I could mention. Some Norfolks like to watch television and one dog in the book used to run behind the set to see where everyone went. (George has actually done this too and once, when a Norfolk screen saver was running on my computer, he squared off and barked furiously at the monitor.) George sounded like one of us right off the bat: problem solvers, not bean counters. We're doers, rebels, artists, relaxed and groovy and terribly inventive.

Training suddenly sounded like fun, especially after my friend Steve in Atlanta, the one who taught his dog to pee on command, told me what a cinch it would be. "Just get a book, any book," Steve said. "Work with the dog ten, fifteen minutes a day and you'll be fine." Steve also told me never to reward George with treats during training, only praise.

How could we miss, with my empathic skills and George's problem-solving abilities? In my mind's eye, I saw the two of us on the Long Meadow, striding along in perfect synchronicity, all the dog people looking at me admiringly and all the dogs lining up to sniff George's butt as he executes a perfect cartwheel in exchange for a soulful pat on the head from me, firm but gentle guardian, Frank Buck meets St. Francis of Assisi.

With time and perspective, I can now see that Steve was lying, lying, lying through his teeth, especially the part about not rewarding with food. I may have taught George very little indeed, but he does know the difference between fine words and biscuits. Praise and other forms of empty rhetoric impress George little. But I took Steve's advice to heart and soon had a shelf of training manuals, enough to fill me with energizing feelings of ignorance and inadequacy. Surely, I thought, all the dog people who came before didn't have to face this burden of research. Actually, they didn't.

"Pet ownership as we know it today is a post–World War II phenomenon," Andrew Rowan of the Humane Society has written, and so is obedience training. The ASPCA began offering free obedience classes for the burgeoning American pet dog population in 1947. Around the same time, the trainer Blanche Saunders traveled the country with her poodles doing obedience demonstrations. They even performed in the skating rink at Rockefeller Center.

Despite such efforts, obedience training for dogs has never caught on in this country. The estimates I've seen of dog owners who do any training beyond housebreaking varies between 5 or 6 and 30 percent. That's not a lot of well-behaved dogs.

However, you would never know this from the number of guides and manuals that are falling off the shelves in your local bookstore. Occasionally one becomes a bestseller, such as *How to Be Your Dog's Best Friend* by the Monks of New Skete. Some of them have been there awhile, such as *The Koehler Method of Dog Training*, continuously in print since 1962. William R. Koehler trained thousands of dogs and handlers for the military during World War

II (as did the trainers of Rin Tin Tin and Lassie), then came home and employed the same principles to train pets. His technique is based largely on negative reinforcement. There's lots of punishment and correction, little empathy. Learning happens as a means of avoiding punishment. Check out the readers' comments about it on Amazon.com or in newsgroups. Forty-plus years after it was written, people are swearing by this book or at it. How many books of similar vintage can provoke such response?

There's no way I could treat Georgie the way Koehler recommends, so I'm glad that today's crop of guides offers kinder, gentler training systems, encouraging positive reinforcement and reward over correction and discipline. One of the least known may be one of the most popular. *There Are No Bad Dogs* (not to be confused with *No Bad Dogs* by Barbara Woodhouse, the voluble Brit who gave the dog world its rallying cry, "Walkies!") sells for $1.19 and you can't buy it at bookstores, only supermarkets and drugstores. Written by Donald W. Denoff, D.V.M., it's been published at least four times in the last decade, and each print run was about 680,000 copies. More exact figures are unavailable, since the publisher,

American Media Mini Mags of Boca Raton, Florida, had to relocate after an anthrax scare in 2002. The company papers are still in the contaminated building.

The language of dog training was new and strange to me. I had never thought about the difference between correction and punishment, reward and reinforcement, except during a course I took on the Russian novel in college. Undeterred, I started with *The Art of Raising a Puppy* by the Monks of New Skete in upstate New York. This was an ecumenical gesture on my part, given that my feelings about both monks and German shepherds (its main subject) are nothing if not complex. *The Art of Raising a Puppy* is the follow-up to *How to Be Your Dog's Best Friend*, the book which espoused the alpha roll, the act of flipping a dog forcibly onto its back and holding it there, proving conclusively that you are top dog. The technique proved controversial, because it gets some dogs so freaked out that they bite. It's since been repudiated by the monks.

I didn't know an alpha roll from a kaiser roll, but I found the book clear-eyed and persuasive, though there wasn't much to take from a book about bringing shepherd puppies into the world to the task of training a year-old terrier who was already housebroken but had never been on a leash. Still, I might have stayed with the monks longer had I not visited their Web site and read about their "New York–style cheesecake," which deep-sixed in a flash any faith I'd had in their training concepts. If they think New York–style cheesecake has Kahlúa in it, what can they know about dogs? Sheesh.

I picked the next guide, *Smarter than You Think* by Paul Loeb and Suzanne Hlavacek, because it looked easy. Fulsome testimonials on the back cover promised great results fast, really fast, with minimal tedious repetition. You don't have to have special words or gestures or tones of voice. And once you've trained your dog, you can stop. "Don't keep insisting," the author counseled. I liked the sound of it. I wanted to believe.

The core of the program is the "Magic Touch." The Magic Touch is a gesture of mystical and mythic power, if you're a dog. If you're not a dog, it is what you bestow on your dog when you give a command and are not obeyed. The Magic Touch is throwing something at your dog. And not too softly, either. Don't throw anything hard or heavy; a ball of socks or an old

160

rubber ball will do. Once the dog realizes that you have the ability to strike it from afar, your sway will be absolute and with no need for reinforcement. And that's that. Simple, no? Forever in thrall to your opposable thumbs, your dog is now ready to learn how to mix daiquiris and juggle. If I recall the book correctly, there was this pair of giant schnauzers who were taking swimming lessons as well as learning Italian.

I don't want to malign the author, who has many fans claiming success on Amazon.com. But for one such as I there are flaws inherent in the system. Flaw 1: I'm not saying I throw like a girl, but no one will ever mistake me for Roger Clemens. It can take me quite a while to hit George from distances of over ten feet. If I stand much closer than that, it's hard to say if he's coming on my command, because he's almost here. When I do manage to hit him, the contact is feeble and glancing, and George regards it as an accident, the harmless by-product of some inscrutable behavior, though certainly no less inscrutable than much of what he sees me do. I often wonder, for example, what George thinks about when he watches with evident fascination as I vigorously exercise on my

NordicTrack. Talk about sound and fury signifying nothing.

Eventually I overcame my mound jitters and connected on a nifty two-seam slider low and away, using a sidearm motion. The balled-up Burlington Mills socks hit George solidly on his left flank. He stopped what he was doing and walked over to me.

I was so dumbfounded that I executed a perfect sit. George wandered off. I threw again, more softly because I was using one of George's piebald tennis balls, and connected with his rump. And again he turned and came to me, stood there for a minute and strolled off. I got the socks again and went into my sidearm windup, but this time George was ready. Just as the socks left my hand he skittered sideways and ran the length of the room, as far from me as he could get. The Magic Touch never worked again and, in fact, plain old "come" didn't, either, as it had during all the weeks we plied him with treats every time he came our way. Which brings us to the second and, in my view, fatal flaw in the Magic Touch system. There is no plan B.

I found out later that, like the New Skete monks, the promulgator of the Magic Touch had likewise changed his views from an earlier book. In 1980's *Supertraining Your Dog*, Paul Loeb recommended such unmagical correctives as putting hot sauce on your dog's gums if she pees on your carpet, accompanied by a firm slap, a practice that violates the Geneva Convention, I believe, let alone the pet-human bond.

My Magic Touch now all o'erthrown, I browsed around lots of other guides, trying out the odd hand signal or clicker approach. Without continuity, there was no effect on George to speak of. Oh, he calmed down and continued to charm us all, including the neighbors, and to establish some nice sniffing relationships with the local dogs. But none of us had any sense that we could get George to do any of the very basic things any training book will tell you are essential. He wouldn't sit, or stay down, didn't really know that's what we were requesting. As for coming when called, forget about it.

I felt completely out of my depth with this small creature. Despite evident goodwill coming from both dog and man, I simply could not make the little bastard do what I wanted him to do. Fortunately or maybe not, there was advice at every goddamn turn.

"You have to pick him up by the scruff

of the neck and hold him at your eye level and let him know who's the alpha," this one fellow on the evening walk circuit tells me. "You look him in the eye and growl." George has a very nice loose scruff and doesn't much mind at all if you pick him up by it. But I don't know about the glare and the growling. I have a hard time growling with a straight face.

In addition to plenty of free advice, my nabe offers many opportunities to learn by observation. One day I was in my local nonsupermarket when a man passed me in the narrow aisle. He was dragging a beaglish dog, and when I say dragging, I mean it. The dog wasn't objecting, or barking, or even moving very much. The dog stood, legs slightly bent and locked into position, like a water-skier behind a motorboat. The guy never even looked back. I felt briefly encouraged; George has never resisted the leash that much. It only feels that way.

My greatest training success on my own was some modest progress with "loose-leash" walking, using the techniques in *Good Owners, Great Dogs* by Brian Kilcommons and Sarah Wilson. It means your dog is walking with you at your pace, not resisting or succumbing to distraction.

Your dog is focused on you and you alone. You and your dog are in sync and you are not afraid to lead. When your dog walks on a loose leash, it means you are a good person.

Even now, when George is much less antsy on the leash than he used to be, the real impediment to the loose-leash thing is that George has never encountered a smell that he didn't want to pursue with every fiber of his densely muscled, furry (hairy?) being. Walking in a straight line with purpose and direction is just not what he does. He's a meanderer. I am not. Compared to George, I am like Roger Bannister pursuing the four-minute mile, or at least a man who likes to walk around the block in less than forty minutes, in a more or less straight line with a few stops to sniff, pee, whatever (that is, the dog does those things, not me). And it goes without saying, except I'm saying it, that I do not want to be whipsawed en route by a little charging demon, lunging under cars to say hi to a cat or diving into promising garbage. My friend Steve says that if I put a choke collar on George, he'll be walking on a loose leash in fifteen minutes. I told him I was not going to put a choke collar on a fifteen-pound dog. "Then you'll be a hundred-eighty-five-pound man getting yanked around by a fifteen-pound dog," Steve said.

The correct number happens to be a hundred seventy-five, but otherwise his description was correct. There are a number of ways of teaching loose-leash walking, and I had applied none of them sufficiently well to have an effect. I needed a class, which is what brought George and family to that dingy church basement.

CLASS ACTION

In order to train a dog, it is imperative to have management and relationship skills.

— Class handout,
Happy Tails Family Dog Training

While most dog owners in this country do no training with their dogs, that is decidedly not the case in the Slope, where puppy obedience classes are as common and competitive as pre-K for toddlers. Classes are particularly effective for dogs who have good study habits and a strong desire to please their people. For George, the benefits were modest.

As a student, George projects an attitude of detached nonchalance, an attitude that asks "What's your problem?" while at the same time hoping for a cookie. It's not that George doesn't want to please us. I'm sure he does, in his way, when he thinks about it. But most of the time, George, like the young Dick Cheney facing military service, has other priorities.

That the class did little for George I mean as no slight to the trainer who ran it, although I must say she has spent what I consider too much time with dogs. Once, I swear, she greeted me with her usual lovely smile and a perky "Up!" She claimed she said "Hi!" but I know what I heard. Still, she knew her stuff and was able to get great results from most of the dogs in our group. And there was no arguing with the basic tenet of her program, which is that dogs will work for food. Ply them with treats and they will do what you want. She rejected the use of choke collars (fine by me, but not feasible for the small woman with the big Lab who sat across from George in class) or even pops of the leash. For best results, she recommended using what are called high-value treats. Feeding

George high-value treats revealed an interspecies bond George and I share: We both love kosher franks, but they don't love us.

The course ended before we could address the cataclysmic digestive aftermath of these training sessions. George wasn't the only one who found the training regimen a bit rich. A young couple in our class took their dog, a rambunctious mix named Brooklyn, for a private training session. On the drive home from the lesson, Brooklyn spewed all over the car. (Brooklyn, by the way, is not an unusual dog name here. Is the same true elsewhere? Are there dogs named Staten, or Manhattan, or Toledo?)

Months after the course was done, I met one of the assistants in the park and suggested that the training traded obedience for obesity. Of course not, she said; the goal is to phase out food rewards by offering them less and less frequently. But she also told me that she and her fellow behaviorists in training are taught, in no uncertain terms, that dogs should leave a basic training class stuffed to the gills.

In effect, the method teaches your dog to play the odds, which is not quite the same as obedience. It's bribery, and it's the reason why, as Brian Kilcommons says, "So many people have to walk around dressed like delis to get their dogs to listen to them." What you want is a dog who responds to you, not the food in your hand. To do that, Kilcommons says, training must address both the behavior you want and your relationship with the animal. "If your dog runs away when you call, that's a relationship problem, not a behavioral one."

George doesn't run away when we call, but he doesn't exactly come right away, either. If I say "Side" while holding a treat, George will come around to my left and sit alongside me, facing in the same direction. Well, it's not exactly right alongside me and he's not really facing the same direction, but he sort of gets the idea that he's supposed to move to my side and sit. That's progress.

There is a difference between behaviors that are annoying — barking at the UPS man — and those that are dangerous. Behaviorist Deborah Manheim says the annoyances she hears about the most are too much barking at the doorbell (I hear you), pulling on the leash (Boy, do I hear), jumping up on people, and stealing items so you'll give chase. Obnoxious as these behaviors are, they are not dangerous.

Biting is in another category. There is little patience in the wider, non–Dog World for dogs that bite or menace.

George is nowhere near dangerous, but after all our efforts with books and with a class, his nipping had yet to be, uh, nipped in the bud. We needed a trainer to work with George and us privately, mano a dogo. We asked around. Everyone recommended the same person.

TYRIL

Don't worry. Help is on the way.

Tyril Frith's answering machine, c. 2002

He is a stocky man with a round shaven head, a gentle manner, and an accent that even many Brooklynites say they can barely understand. It is the lilting patois of the Trinidad countryside, where Tyril Frith was born and lived until he was thirty-three. When he was eight or nine, he got his dog, a mutt a family friend had given him, to fish a cricket ball out of a stream where one of his playmates had dropped it. By fifteen, people were paying him to work with their dogs. He's worked with them more or less ever since.

Tyril has trained dogs for police departments and security companies, and he's been on television with a dog named Sir Oliver Hollywood. If you walk across the Long Meadow when the dog people are out, you will overhear Tyril's name in a half-dozen conversations. Sometimes he's out there, working with a client and shaking hands with others, while their dogs slink around at a discreet distance. But to get the full effect, you have to invite him to meet your dog at home.

George greeted the knock on the door with barking. We leashed him, opened the door, and hoped for the best. Tyril came in and told us to remove the leash. Without raising his arms or eyes, Tyril made his way across the living floor, pointing out to us that he was not threatening or challenging George even as he entered his space. George shadowed him, but kept his distance. Tyril sat at the kitchen table and we arranged ourselves around him. George slipped nimbly by the stranger and slithered behind my son's feet, looking out from around the denim pant legs anxiously, behavior he had never exhibited before or since.

Tyril's methods are his own, though they are not very different from those used by dozens of other trainers and behaviorists. (The difference between a trainer and a behaviorist, by the way, is one of degree: A behaviorist has one and a trainer doesn't. Anyone at all can call himself a dog trainer.) He combines motivational techniques with "corrections," which is what smart trainers dispense now instead of "punishment." The three parts of Tyril's method involve teaching desired behavior, correcting it through negative stimulation to enforce the learning, and finally proofing, which means invoking the behavior in the face of increasing distraction. The principal means of correction is both harmless and terrifying to George. It is the Rattle of Justice.

The Rattle of Justice is an empty plastic water bottle with enough coins in it to produce a robust noise when shaken. The first time Tyril used it, he held it up to George, who stared at it with eyes on stalks. Tyril pressed his mouth against his arm and bleated a short, harsh Bronx cheer. George snorted and backed away. He didn't look angry, he looked scared. Then Tyril took a step closer and threw the thing down right by George. We were all so attuned to the mood by now that everybody jumped, not just the dog.

If all Tyril did was frighten George, his

training wouldn't have amounted to much. Instead, Tyril wove a spell, utterly commanding George's attention. Once, Tyril took an empty black garbage bag and began to walk around the room with it, first flapping it noisily at George, then away. George crept all the way to the other side of the room, right by the staircase and pressed against the wall. I thought he was going to run up to our bedroom and wedge himself into one of his places. But he didn't, and he never took his eyes off Tyril either. He was transfixed.

Sessions with Tyril were always short, never longer than forty minutes or so, and he was careful to stop at the first sign that George was too tired or distracted or upset to be receptive to the training. Within three sessions, a mere jiggle of the rattle was enough to back George away from people coming into our house and even to stay off food on the street. (Since that day, I must confess, the only way I can keep George from eating off the street is the traditional rude yank.) Our mission seemed to be accomplished in remarkably short order.

Tyril suggested we move out to the park, where there are more distractions. He also wanted enough space to teach George a serious come-when-called. I had told Tyril what my friend had said about Norfolks off-leash, but he didn't buy it. And my fear of George unbound was getting embarrassing. Once he slipped out of his harness on the street. I don't think he intended to and I'm not even sure he was aware of what had happened, because I swooped down and scooped him into my arms with such alacrity that other dog people turned their heads. I loudly pretended to be playing with him, whereas I was really afraid he'd run off and I'd never see him again. Another time we were in the park and met Zooey (not Zoe), a stylish little quasi-dachshund in a quilted coat, and Fiona, a sweet Lab with a kerchief around her neck. George was the crossover boy, sniffing Zooey and cantering in circles with Fiona, with whom he would have been hard put to keep up if she hadn't kept getting herself hogtied in George's leash. Zooey's owner, a young mom with a slumbering kid draped around her neck like a wonderful accessory, raised her eyebrows when I explained that I didn't feel I could take George off-leash, even to disentangle Fiona. So that was why I bought a hundred-foot length of string and a thirty-foot training lead and we all went to the park with Tyril.

Brian Kilcommons likes to say that his

training philosophy is that there is no philosophy. The key is in the connection between dog and human. Tyril says, "The important thing is learning to read the dog." Watching Tyril convinces me that training dogs, like any kind of teaching, is more of an art than a science. After three sessions with him and a few weeks of walks with the long lead, George is good to go off-leash — assuming the area is circumscribed, assuming there are no cars, assuming I've got a pocketful of goodies, assuming a lot of things. He will come when called, more or less. I've even successfully called him away from the Sunday-morning-coming-down garbage can overflow in the picnic area once or twice. Watching him hurtling toward me at full gallop never fails to make me grin idiotically and sometimes shout embarrassments like "Good boy! Yee-es!" in precisely the juiced-up tone I have sworn a thousand times I would never adopt. And sometimes when I watch him trotting around companionably with all the morning dogs, I get all wistful the way I expect to be when my son graduates from high school, and I think, "Well, you gotta love 'em and you gotta let 'em go," and then I think, wait, wait, this is the *dog,* not the child.

CITIZEN GEORGE

I am convinced that dogs think humans are nuts.

— John Steinbeck, *Travels with Charley*

George will not be participating in any obedience competitions in the near or remote future. Like my friend Gary, who cannot resist feeding his dog table scraps, I'm not good at imposing obedience on George. In fact, the words "imposing obedience" are distasteful to me. Is this impractical, perhaps even silly? You bet.

Take the loose-leash-walking issue. It would be more easily resolved if we, the three human members of our pack, could settle on a side on which we would all like George to walk when we are walking him. This is called heeling, another word I don't much care for. In the show ring and as per custom, the proper side for heeling is the left, but this need not be the case. Brooklyn, the dog who puked in transit, was being trained to heel on the right. The point is to be consistent. And consistency, at least insofar as it applies to which side the dog should walk on, is just not hap-

176

pening in this family. Two of us are left-handed, one's a righty. Sometimes you've got groceries in one hand or the other. Sometimes there's foot traffic. I mean, who can be bothered figuring out which god-damn side George should walk on? And then training him to do it, so he'll never again know what it feels like to walk on the other side of whoever's walking him? It's not fair to him and it's not fair to us. Spending one whit of time figuring out which side we'd like George to walk on for the rest of his days, let alone training him to do so, seems like sheer idiocy to me. At least we don't have to drag him behind us, like the floor-skimming beagle in the bodega.

I have taught George to sit, wait, and catch small treats that I throw to him from distances approaching fifteen feet, a stunt that never fails to attract admiring stares from the passing throng. Once I went out with a blue miniature tennis ball, thinking I could leverage the biscuit-catching trick into learning to catch and fetch. I held up the ball just as I do with treats and said, "Georgie . . . catch!" as I threw it gently up toward him.

It was a perfect throw, right to him but with enough arc to allow him time to pre-pare, so I was very surprised when George sat there while the ball bonked him on his adorable snout. I apologized, retrieved the ball, and started again. I put George into a sit, which is to say I said "Sit" and he actually sat. I backed away, holding up the ball and giving the breathless command "Catch!" This time he ran away as soon as I released the ball, which fell squarely on the spot where he would have been. Enough for today, I thought, and extracted a biscuit fragment from my pocket. I held it up to show him and said, "Okay, back to normal, Georgie. Sit. Stay . . . catch!" and he ran away.

One morning in the park, I was handed a circular by a park volunteer. It read:

IS YOUR DOG SOCIALLY ACCEPTABLE?

Mine is!!
Kings County Kennel Club
Canine Good Citizenship Testing
Sunday May 18th
Wollman Rink in Prospect Park
Mixed Breeds Welcome . . .

A noncompetitive test for owners to show that their dogs have passable social manners and are able to perform some simple tasks like be able to sit or stand while a stranger pats him. You will be judged as a team. Sponsored by the Kings County Kennel Club: A must for all dogs who frequent Prospect Park and beyond. Entry Fee: $10/dog.

Owners must bring current rabies Vaccination Certificate, Dog License, and a grooming brush or comb. Dogs must be on-leash at all times.

Da noive. The very title annoyed me. I'm supposed to pay some clubhouse martinet to pass judgment on George? Not that George couldn't handle whatever was required. And what's the deal with the grooming comb? My dander was up, and I knew we'd be there on the day.

The Canine Good Citizenship Tests are part of Prospect Park's Summer You Gotta Have Park festival, when the whole place is bustling with special events like children's theaters and birding walks. All the precious, newly restored bits of the park that have been closed for renovation are cleaned up and opened to the public. So it hardly seemed fair that the damn dog tests were held on the flat concrete slab of the out-of-season Wollman Ice Skating Rink, which is not only a very long walk from my house, but was at the time perhaps the ugliest place in the park.

I'd forgotten what it felt like to walk George for a long time on a leash. How it felt was not so good. He pulled all the time and there were very few other dogs about for quick sniffing interludes. And so many people. I passed children's puppeteers on their break, freelance percussionists jamming with the kids who were waiting for the puppeteers to get back from their breaks, Frisbee games, drumming circles, and lots and lots of picnics.

I knew I must be getting close when I passed a young guy with an antic pug with whom George briefly communed. The guy clutched something that looked like a receipt and various dog-related information packets. He had good hair and a suede jacket and he was having an animated conversation on his cell. "Oh, yes, I was in the drama club in high school. I think all gay men are in the drama club in high school, because that's always the only place where you can be around other gay men."

The Good Citizen testing folks look like they'd had a hard day waiting for throngs that never showed up while they passed the best part of a glorious day in this dreary spot.

Still, serious dog people are nothing if not enthusiastic, so as George and I approached, a woman with a Minnie Pearl–type Southern accent cried out, "A terrier! Hot damn! How about that! Does the man have nerve or what!"

"He's adorable," said another woman with a clipboard. "We haven't had any terriers in here today."

"Except Louie in the ring now," said Minnie Pearl. "He's got some terrier in there."

I looked at Louie. He probably did have some terrier in there, and every other kind of dog, too. Alongside the flat gray rink were a few benches and a couple of dogs. A long lean gent with a perfect silver-gray pompadour and skinny black clothes smoked extra-long cigarettes, stroked his borzoi, and talked about breeding. If the Sopranos ever go into the kennel business, they should get this guy. A young man with an enormous chow encouraged his dog as she shook out her bushy coat. "Shakesshake! Shakeshake! She likes to be clean, don't you, girl? Shakeshake!"

The citizenship test itself was somewhat of an anticlimax after the walk to reach it. George and I stood in the rink and executed various simple commands. They told

181

me to tell George to sit, I told George to sit, he sat. And so on, making George sit, then walking away twenty feet or so and calling him. Things could have gotten dicier when the other dog entered the arena, but the dog who was working these tests was so docile and unaggressive that he and George passed each other with a cursory sniff the first time and the second time, when they were supposed to behave while the other walker and I stop and talked, both dogs lay down on the asphalt.

For the finale, George had to do something I was sure he couldn't manage. I had to hand the leash to the evaluator, who led George out of the ring and behind a barricade, so that I was out of his sight. Then he had to behave, maybe do a sit or something, for a minute or two. Then I had to call him.

Tyril taught George to come when called by holding him and ordering us to walk away. The drive not to be separated from us was the way he learned the behavior. Would he let himself be led away this time?

He did. And he came when I called. A month later we received a felt patch and a certificate of citizenship for George. George himself received a card from an officer of the Kings County Kennel Club asking if he'd consider running for office.

That was the high-water mark of George's career in obedience. Since then, he's gotten mellower, but not appreciably more eager to please. Dogs are said to thrive on training, so it's possible I'm the one with the authority problem, not George. But if I want to pursue an enrichment program, there is, lord knows, no dearth.

5. busy dogs

GEORGE'S GIG

Asking a working writer what he thinks about critics is like asking a lamppost what it feels about dogs.

— John Osborne

Joining the Dog World has meant more reading than I'd anticipated. One of my favorite works is a brief article called "Entertaining Your Norfolk Terrier" by Sheila Foran. It can be found, unsurprisingly, on the Web site of the America Norfolk Terrier Association. I like the article for two reasons: First, you can tell from the title that the author has her priorities straight. Second, it makes me feel that our stewardship of George is probably pretty good, or at least entertaining. Sheila Foran suggests walks morning or evening; George gets both those and more. She suggests teaching your Norfolk tricks; we've certainly taught George tricks. His learning them is another matter. We demur on Ms. Foran's suggestion of taking George for rides in the car to wade in a nearby stream. Riding in the car makes George vomit sometimes, and the nearest stream reachable by car in these parts is the fetid, although rapidly gentrifying, Gowanus Canal.

If someone had presented my father-in-law with a document entitled "Entertaining Your Cocker Spaniel," he would have laughed and assumed the thing was written by an American. He knew perfectly well what entertained Kim, but Kim's amusement was not the point of the exercise. Kim was the right dog for the job. His role as family pet was an extra.

By contrast, the Long Meadow in the morning is full of hunting dogs, tracking dogs, herding dogs, and fighting dogs with nothing to hunt, track, herd, or fight, and people who are trying to make it up to them. Retrievers retrieve tennis balls instead of pheasant. Herders herd other dogs or human dawdlers holding insulated coffee mugs. Caring owners wield Chuck-Its ("Never bend over to pick up a slobbery ball again!") so their Weimaraners and poodle-shepherd-Lab-whatevers can gallop after far-flung tennis balls. Occasionally a beefy pit mix will promenade down the meadow with a tree-size branch clasped in powerful jaws, dogs and people moving out of the wide load's path. The owners of the enormous Scottish deerhound, Terry, who is unneutered, keep him away from crowded parts of the meadow on weekend mornings, lest the enormous, medieval-looking animal forget his manners. Once I saw a German short-haired pointer actually pointing, though at what was not clear. Another time a couple of doughty corgis (and what corgis aren't?) started circling a cluster of buff Rhodesian ridgebacks who didn't take kindly to the flanking maneuvers. The owners took note, and a ridgey-corgi rumble was narrowly averted.

George's life is, I believe and hope, a happy one so far, but it is not the life for which his bloodlines, the generations of cute little red-brown dogs that came before him, are supposed to have prepared him. That would be a life in which he'd "go to ground, bolt a fox and tackle or dispatch other small vermin, working alone or with a pack," as described in the AKC breed standard. George's life is just not, by that or any other measure, Norfolkian.

I'd be delighted if George became our ratter, mouser, scourge of vole and shrew; though city rats would be a stretch for George, and I'm not sure where you find vole and shrew around here. Nonetheless, George-appropriate prey flourishes in these parts, as you'd think his encounters with the victims of our mousetraps would have taught him. But no such luck. As I write, there is another mouse, a live one, residing in our kitchen. For two weeks it has resisted the blandishments of numerous traps baited with organic peanut butter and artisanal cheese. The mouse has not only resisted them; I recently entered the kitchen to find the tiny fellow making himself a lettuce and tomato sandwich on our kitchen counter. Well, not exactly, but the mouse was in no hurry. George was there, too. He saw the mouse when I did, stood alert for a moment, and then ambled over to his squeak toy, while the mouse retreated in leisurely fashion, dragging off the good scotch as he went. One night in our backyard, when the local bullfrog was in particularly full-throated song using what my wife calls his "port-breath voice," George cowered by a shrub. He accidentally caught a goldfish in our water feature once, then looked at it flopping on the bluestone until it flopped back in the water. More often he just leans and leans a little farther in each time, watching, until he falls in and has to struggle to the shore and come to terms with his embarrassment, which doesn't take long.

George is very fond of water he has not fallen into by accident. His favorite water is the kind that comes out of a faucet or hose. If I'm trying to amuse him on a hot summer's day without actually having to do anything myself, I always go for the hose option. He leaps and dashes madly in and out of the stream and sometimes turns directly into it, so he gets the full force of the water pressure. Once he sprained his toe doing that, causing all of us to reflect on our leisure choices.

Fortunately, George has other aquatic opportunities. He is a seasonal regular at Prospect Park's famous Dog Beach, although, like all metro area beaches, it is overcrowded at peak hours. Best of all, though, is the shower.

I'm told George is one of the few dogs who enjoys taking showers. When we return from a walk in the rain, George impatiently waits for me to hang up my Gore-Tex before spritzing me with one of his full-body shakes, the one piece of doggish behavior I truly wish I could emulate. Then he hurtles up the stairs and into the bathroom to sit by the tub, waiting for me to follow. Sometimes I prolong the moment, mounting the stairs and walking past the bathroom door a couple of times without entering. George drops his hints — looking at me, then at the tub, then at me, then at the tub. If I pause in the doorway long enough, he rises and puts his front paws on the bath mat folded over the side of the tub. Sometimes he tries to jump into the tub, but he hasn't managed it yet. I have to place him in and turn the faucets. Georgie jumps at the flow, drinks, soaks his head, and then, to his immense delight, intently studies the water as it circles and goes down the drain. If his undercarriage is muddy, I use the hair-washing handle attachment to hose away the dirt. Then I leave him there. He's stayed in the tub as long as two hours, and he never looks less than utterly fascinated by what he's doing. Once, when my wife wanted to lift him out before he was ready, he nipped at her hand — gently, of course.

Adorable as this is, I'm forced to adapt ruses when I take a shower, or George will try to join me. There is a certain charm to this, but if you've ever accidentally stepped on a small dog when you both have soap in your eyes, you will know that it's not unmitigated fun. So I try to lure him to another floor, out of hearing range, before I turn on the faucet. But on more than one occasion, he's heard the slap of water on tile and he's back, paws up on the edge of the tub if I've forgotten to close the bathroom door, hurling himself against it if I have. Eventually the sound of his full-body attacks subsides and by the time I emerge, he's curled in front of the door, wan, resigned, and, it seems to me, obscurely hurt. I don't know how I can explain to George why my showering needs are different from, and in some ways exclusive of, his own.

If George is not sleeping, he can amuse himself for only so long before he gets bored, very bored. And, while figuring out what captivates George can be puzzling at times, figuring out that he's bored is a slam-dunk. I mean, if his toys, favored lolling areas (under the big chair in the living room, on his "special chair," and ten or twelve other locations), and patrolling the garden start to pall, he lets me know. You know how. The stare.

Sure I've already mentioned it, but I don't think you realize its power. It is a reserved yet imploring look, bottomless brown eyes rimmed by extravagant brows that seem to focus his gaze. He tilts his head to one side, then the other. Sometimes, the worst times, he accompanies his plangent gazes with high-pitched whinnying sounds that are not quite as annoying as the sounds Lassie made, but very nearly.

It is a look that forces one to ask the toughest of tough questions: Am I entertaining my Norfolk terrier?

Before I know it, I'm lost in a brown (reddish-brown) study, wondering again about George's idea of Nirvana. What could he want that he doesn't have in Brooklyn? Here he has plenty of walks, unlimited drain-watching, a yard to mess around in, cool tiles, and cozy cushions for snoozing. If that isn't enough, don't forget the day-care crowd. Would he be happier in Norfolk or even Norwich? I doubt it. I drove through Norwich once. Like most cities viewed from a car, it looked like a traffic jam. We have those here. Still, I know I would be a better dog person if I really invested some time in an activity that George and I could share.

George can't be the only Norfolk alienated from his own instincts, I thought as I wended my way through the countryside roads to Green Village, New Jersey, where the American Norfolk Terrier Association Spring Antic was in full swing. I didn't bring George because I thought we'd both feel uncomfortable, but the antic turns out to be a casual event. There are Norfolk races (very short, very funny) and a groomer, around whom people stand in awed silence as she gradually reveals the contours of a petite dog that had arrived on the grooming table looking like a thatched roof.

Susan Ely, a Norfolk breeder and trainer whose dogs compete both in the show ring and in earth-dog competitions, was preparing for a demonstration of the latter, to which all dogs on hand were invited to participate. As you know, the word "terrier" comes from *terra,* the Latin word for "earth" — not, as the venerable Dog World joke has it, the Latin word for "terror." Earth-dog training is all about developing terrierish skills by exciting the animals' prey drive. That's why Susan Ely was holding a caged black rat; it was the motivation.

If someone were to walk into my house with a black rat in a cage, there's a good chance I'd jump atop the nearest settee and shriek. If I were wearing crinolines, I'd lift them. But in the Dog World, rats are just part of life's rich pageant. Susan Ely put the rat down to set up a series of wooden passages so people could take turns letting their dogs zip down the little tunnels to the cage. Between turns, Ely connected more passages, end to end, to make the prey harder to get to. Some dogs gave up inside and backed out. Others lost interest entirely. One woman kept cheering her Norfolk on by calling "Get-rat-Get-rat-GET-RAT!" but her little dog just wasn't into rats that day. One dog went absolutely nuts and had to be yanked away. The rat, by the way, remained out of reach of the cute terriers, to serve another day as bait. That rat has a bad job.

Ever since that demonstration, I've been promising myself that I'm going to take George to something similar, but it hasn't happened. I suspect the reason for my failure to do so is the hidden fear that he might turn out to like it. How great would that be, having to bring home feeder mice just to keep his prey instinct honed? I'm sure there must be an activity that will bring George and me closer together without requiring him to learn to read or me to bring home feeder mice. If there's an answer to be found anywhere, it's at Crufts.

CORNUCOPIA

Whatever competition you choose, your dog will be a happier pet for being trained.

— from *Crufts Dog Days Out* beginner's guide

Here's a partial list of the activities you could see at just one of the 30-odd show rings at the 101st Crufts Kennel Club All Breed Dog Show in Birmingham, England:

Heelwork to Music
Pro Plan Protection Team
Rescue Dog Agility
HM Customs and Excise
Eukanuba Invitation Mini Pairs
Canine Partners Display
Southern Golden Retriever Society
Flyball Semifinals
Safe and Sound Display
Paws for Thought Display Team
Tricky Tykes Terrier Display Team
West Midlands Police Displays

You can also find dancing dogs, agility pugs (irony rather than athleticism was their shtick), as well as the Discover Dogs booths, the Scotland Yard trainers, and the field trial people.

Although it is frequently spoken of as the British equivalent of Westminster, Crufts is very different in tone and scope. It has ten times as many dogs, about 25,000 to Westminster's 2,500. They must all have won a certain number of points to qualify, but, unlike Westminster entrants, they needn't be finished champions. In fact, it is relatively easy to accumulate enough points to enter Crufts, especially if yours is an unusual breed and you live where there aren't very many others. Because it is by qualification, rather than invitation, there are far more nonprofessionals here, pure enthusiasts who enjoy the competition. In the opinion of some, that lowers the standard. I overheard an Old English sheepdog aficionado refer to one group winner as "the most unsound dog I've seen in a ring in twenty years."

"You see a lot of junk here, because you can get in with just a couple of small wins," Barbara Miller told me. But she also thinks the problem is one of style as well as substance. "We do it better in the States. We groom better, we show better, our handlers are better. Here they just schlep 'em around the ring." Of course, Britain is terrier country, even if one of the dogs who placed was from Norway and had an undocked tail, as required by Norwegian law but frowned on by classicists like Barbara. Barbara approved of some of the dogs she saw, but only narrowly. "The dogs that won in each Norfolk class were the only ones worth looking at."

For four days, Crufts utterly dominates its environment like no dog show could ever dominate New York City. For four days, the headline of the *Birmingham Post and Mail* is a variant of BACKUPS ON THE M-42 WILL RUIN OUR REPUTATION! The trains to and from the show were packed at all times, and sometimes it seemed that the entire population of Britain was shuffling around with me in the immense halls of Birmingham's National Exhibition Center, ogling the dogs.

I'd wanted to visit Crufts because it is the biggest dog show in the world, but I learned it's much more than that. It's a loose, informative, vast forum for all the ways people have found to share life with their dogs. As I ambled around drinking it all in, I felt guiltier and guiltier about all that George and I were not doing.

I chatted with a young police officer who's involved in Scotland Yard's breeding program. I watched women train hunting dogs. I learned that heelwork to music, which is dancing with your dog, takes a lot more effort to master than you might think — which distinguishes it from canine freestyle, a looser, more anarchic American variant that is to heelwork to music as hoedown time is to *Riverdance*. I spent hours in the Discover Dogs area, where breed clubs maintain little stalls with a couple of dogs and endless information sheets. I bonded immediately with the folks manning the Norfolk stall, and one of them promised to send me a copy of Martin Phillips's famous video, *How to Groom Your Norfolk Terrier*, that would be playable on American VCRs (I'm still waiting, Valerie). I noticed one snapshot that really looked like George, then noticed it was a picture demonstrating a "blown coat," which you know isn't good. I discussed the undocked Norwegian dog and got the feeling no one liked the look. "It's not in proportion" was the dour view I heard repeatedly.

Tail docking began as a way to distinguish working dogs, which were not taxed, from pets, which were. Aesthetic considerations were a distinct afterthought. I decided not to make any circumcision jokes, which was probably wise since it was England, and moved on.

I returned to my hotel after each day of Crufts bearing merchandise and freebies: kibble samples, a book, a laminated picture of a Norfolk captioned "Warning! Intruders will be licked to death," a rubber Crufts trophy that squeaks, and tons of pamphlets, booklets, and dog data sheets. I've kept them all. It is thanks to that trove of information that I can intelligently discuss the developmental history of the Hamiltonstovarë (like a beagle, but bigger), the learning skills of the puli, and the exciting work being done to reestablish the bergamasco, a thickly corded Italian sheepdog that is rarer than the giant panda.

I'm sure I like the idea of George and me doing heelwork to music more than I would like the amount of time it would take to get him to weave between my legs as I walked in rhythm to, say, "Walk on the Wild Side." And that's just one move. You've got to fill a whole song. Given both George's and my shared revulsion to rodents, I don't think earth dog has much future. Obedience? Don't be ridiculous. Agility? George is certainly agile. But the curious thing about agility as a form of training and competition is that it is no way, shape, or form instinctive for any dog. No dog will go over an obstacle if going around it is an option. I can't see myself negotiating that with George. Most competitive dog events depend more on control and discipline than on what dogs do naturally. Racing is different.

I'VE GOT THE DOG RIGHT HERE

Mention the words "Greyhound Racing" and, for many, it conjures up thoughts of men in flat caps or shady characters in sharp suits with a sly cigarette dangling from the corner of their mouths. . . . Modern-day greyhound racing has shaken off its dusty old image, and "a night at the dogs" now provides a most enjoyable evening's entertainment. Plush restaurants, corporate entertainment facilities, private boxes, and clean, well-run bars are the face of greyhound racing in the new millennium and the sport attracted a new kind of clientele.

— www.4dogracing.com

Long before George came along, I dreamed of being a shady character in a sharp suit, so you could say that my interest in dog racing follows from my interest in menswear. My curiosity was further piqued by the dapper remake of *Ocean's Eleven*, in which shady George Clooney and sharp Brad Pitt meet briefly at a dog track to exchange expository mumblings. I hoped that I might find remnants or hints of a lost world there: Guys and Dolls and Dogs, colorful characters circulating around the betting windows, legendary dogs, knowledgeable fans.

As any greyhound enthusiast will tell you, greyhounds are an ancient breed renowned for speed and hunting prowess. They are said to have existed 4,000 years ago, back when they should've been wolves. And all that time, they've been racing. Egyptians raced greyhounds. So did Queen Elizabeth I, in whose honor greyhound racing became known as the Sport of Queens.

The sport the Egyptians and Elizabeth enjoyed was coursing, the pursuit of live game — a rabbit, a fox — over open country. First hound to catch the prey had first crack at lunch. Coursing after a mechanical lure is still practiced, but modern greyhound racing, dogs dashing a fixed distance around an oval track in pursuit of a plastic bag or a scrap of fur, didn't become popular until the 1920s.

Just as the sport is different, so are the dogs.

The greyhound of antiquity was a distinctly slimmer creature than the current model. But starting in 1770, one Lord Orford began crossing greyhounds with English bulldogs. If this sounds like an unfortunate marriage, keep in mind that bulldogs of the day were slimmer and more muscular, rather like today's bull terriers. Lord Orford's dogs kept their sleek greyhound shape but developed greater strength and power, a clear instance of hybrid vigor. Today's deep-chested speed demons, capable of reaching 45 mph on a straightaway, are descended from Orford's dogs. This is not your medieval ancestor's greyhound. And while it's questionable whether having an instinct to chase something is the same as loving to chase it, I wanted to see those dogs run.

It turns out that dog tracks are in places like Hindale, New Hampshire, Revere, Massachusetts, Council Bluffs, Iowa, locales unevocative of Sky Masterson, Lady Luck, or Lord Orford. The quickest, closest action I could find was in Colt's

Neck, New Jersey, a meet sponsored by the Garden State Sighthounds Association in accordance with the rules of NOTRA, the National Oval Track Racing Association. It's not the only racing organization around. There's also the WRA (Whippet Racing Association), LGRA (Large Gazehound Racing Association), and ASFA (American Sighthound Field Association), among many others. They stage amateur races for sighthound breeds. There is no betting and no animal cruelty, and there are no animal rights demonstrators, either.

Colt's Neck is yet another of the tony New Jersey precincts I have come to visit since George. The crowd was more mixed than the neighborhood. Alongside the customary tweedy folk in their waxed cotton jackets and Wellies and the soccer moms with minivans full of borzoi stood a scruffy young guy with a bandanna covering a receding hairline. When the talk turned to dog food, he proudly said he fed his whippet Purina.

People who get up early to race their dogs on a Saturday morning that isn't very warm are, ipso facto, hard-core dog people. Conversation was spirited.

"A whippet bitch will run your home."

"A whippet bitch *does* run my home."

"My alpha whippet bitch tells all the other dogs in the house and the cats where to go. She'll just stand in the doorway and arch her back and the other dogs will go around her."

"And yet she'll never put a mark on anyone."

"Absolutely. She does it all with *presence.*"

Some salukis are howling in their crates. The "oval track" is really a field with a Gyro Gearloose–like motor in the middle, from which comes a cord that is wrapped around an oval of divots. The motor huffs and puffs and pulls a plastic "rabbit" around the circuit. The dogs are placed in a starting box, which is opened when the rabbit zooms by.

A quartet of beefy Rhodesian ridgebacks makes a stately circuit. Even though we're in New Jersey, the basenjis are clearly not born to run. Two of them lose interest before they make a full circuit, and the third foolishly tries to attack a greyhound who has broken away from its owners and is thundering across the track toward the plastic rabbit. The real action is whippets and greyhounds. When the greyhounds race, mighty pumping hindquarters, front legs at full stretch just like the dog on the side of a Greyhound bus, they are something to see.

I recognized a couple of dogs from the park. The Intrepid Greyhounds of Brooklyn, Blade and Haley, have their own Web site. Blade was the top-ranked NOTRA greyhound last year, and Haley the second-ranked LGRA greyhound. When I usually see them, they are nosing around the debris under the picnic tables while their owner, Tracy Rudsitas, makes hopeful noises.

These graceful dogs inspire devotion. In college, Tracy developed a fascination with them despite, or perhaps because of, having grown up with a succession of Irish setters who were all named Kelly. A couple of years later, she adopted a retired brindled greyhound and named her Niagara.

Blade and Haley have a very busy schedule during racing season. For the better part of six months, Tracy spends her weekends at lure-coursing or track meets. She told me she will probably always have greyhounds.

Bonnie Dalzell's home page displays a picture of a six-legged dog over a caption that reads, "Advances in Biotechnology create new opportunities for dog breeders!"

The home page of her kennel, Silkenswift, is more serious. Since 1976, Silkenswift has produced more performance-titled sighthounds (mostly borzoi, but also salukis) than any kennel in the world. This has won the honor and respect of her peers in the purebred borzoi world.

As we say in Brooklyn, that and two bucks will buy her a token for the subway. That's not true anymore, because tokens are no longer accepted in New York subways, but my point is the same. Silkenswift is a labor of love that grew out of Bonnie's intellectual curiosity. "I got into raising dogs because I was doing a Ph.D. in biomechanics and I figured out that what I was doing could help dogs run faster. And they've always done well. . . . If I'd raised greyhounds I'd have made much more money." Breeders move in mysterious ways.

As much as I enjoyed watching the dogs run at Colt's Neck, I wondered if they were bush leaguers compared to pari-mutuel track dogs. So I went down to Derby Lane Dog Track in St. Petersburg, Florida, in June 2003, to attend the closing weekend's festivities before the dogs moved across the Howard Franklin Causeway for the following week's season opener at the Tampa Greyhound Track.

Established in 1925, Derby Lane is the oldest dog track in the country and is still owned by the family that founded it. In its heyday, Derby Lane boasted visitors like Errol Flynn, Joe DiMaggio, and Babe Ruth.

Greyhound racing today is an industry in serious decline, hard hit by competition from casinos and other gambling venues and by political pressure from animal activists. Today there are thirty tracks scattered across fifteen states, all of them routinely picketed and petitioned by activist groups.

Although the *Ocean's Eleven* scene was filmed at Derby Lane, Brad and George, not to mention Errol and the Babe, would have stood out like sore thumbs amid today's clientele. The last celebrity I've heard of visiting a dog track was Pete Rose. Derby Lane today is a haunt for old gents in comfortable shoes and matching belts, and father-and-son Hell's Angels, not to mention the broads in their cutoffs and espadrilles and halter tops, clutching Newports, wallet, and car keys in a bunched fist. Florida seems to have an unlimited number of these women in virtually every age bracket, and they all seem to have great legs, no matter what else has happened to them. Notwithstanding the high-quality gams, it was not what you'd consider a high-octane crowd.

In fact, there didn't seem to be much of a crowd at all, nothing like the number of people I'd judged would be there from the cars in the lot. The widely spaced rows of benches lining the track were almost empty. The bar's long wraparound counter was sparsely populated. Not many hot dogs or fries were being bought. Here it was, a beautiful day, sunny and sultry with just enough breeze and overcast moments to keep it interesting. But in Florida, the kind of weather that can make a visitor weep with pleasure is exactly the kind the locals ignore.

Most of the folks at Derby Lane were inside, where there's air-conditioning, and the races can be watched on ubiquitous TV monitors. In the tiered main dining room overlooking the track, there's a roast beef buffet for a very reasonable price and a monitor on every table. One room is set aside for low-stakes poker, which is very popular, but the monitors are never far away. They're showing Derby Lanes races and much more: greyhound races in Jacksonville and Pensacola, big-league baseball, basketball, horse racing, and the ever-popular jai alai, which persists in the unlikeliest places for a sport of Basque origin.

A greyhound race is over in a few seconds, so a good deal of the experience is foreplay. Each race is separated by longueurs in which the regulars consult the inscrutable fine print of their programs and place their bets. The track at Derby Lane encircles a tropical tableau: fountain, waterfall, palm trees. Between races, a sort of Zamboni for dirt drags a grooming rake around the oval, while the hounds wait to make their entrance in a little building that is open on one side down at the far end of the oval. This is the weighing room. Visitors are allowed to watch the weigh-in, but the handlers ("leadouts" in track parlance) are not allowed to talk or communicate in any way with them. It could be construed as tampering with the races, so most studiously avoid eye contact. At the appointed hour, the leadouts lead the dogs out, over a footbridge and onto the dirt track itself, then to the edge of the track facing the stands.

The dogs are beautiful in their bright racing silks, pawing the ground and stretching their slim necks. Several of them choose this moment in the spotlight to do what comes naturally. As is so often the case with bodily functions, there's a ripple effect, and not just among the dogs. Once one greyhound starts pooping and others follow suit, there is a surge at the betting windows. These are the gamblers with theories: the dog who poops first wins, the dog who poops last wins, the dog who holds it in has that edge of urgency.

Racing greyhounds rarely travel to different venues, the way horses do. They spend most of their careers in residence at one track or another. The greyhounds at Derby Lane are there for the six-month season, then they go to Tampa. They race two to three times a week. In all that time, you would think they'd cotton to the fact that it's not a real rabbit, wouldn't you? Maybe they have, but just can't resist the rush. Besides, hope springs eternal, doesn't it? Just look at the lines at the betting windows.

A day at the dog track is a lot of fun for not much money. Parking is free, admission is minimal, a beer is about three bucks. In a typical day, there are fifteen or so races. That's an inexpensive way to spend a few hours, unless you gamble, which most people are there to do, and which can make a day at the dogs costly.

You will understand what kind of gambler I am when I tell you that for a quick trip to St. Pete in June, I brought a sweater. All my gambling during my day at the races was governed by the I-like-the-name principle. After a win that netted me a big seven and change, I found myself parsing the hieroglyphs in the program for hints as to which dog would get to the rubber bunny first. My final bet was on a quiniela, which I had previously thought to be a Mexican baked good, but which turns out to be a way to bet on three dogs at once and still lose. Down by a sawbuck, I didn't feel at all like Sky Masterson. I felt like that guy who gives Tony Soprano his kid's SUV.

Even if you don't think, as I do, that gambling is mostly a tax on people who can ill afford it, there's no getting away from the bottom line of the greyhound industry. The tracks need lots of dogs, but not for life. In 2002 a former security guard at the Pensacola Greyhound Track named Richard Rhodes was arrested after aerial photographs revealed piles of bones littering his eighteen-acre spread. The man had been executing old racing dogs on his property for a standard rate of ten dollars per dog. It was part-time work, and he'd been doing it ever since he got out of high school. At the time of his arrest, he was sixty-eight. Incidents like this, and there are plenty of them, cloud the future of parimutuel tracks.

I feel certain that the people I met at Derby Lane don't mistreat dogs. The kennel I saw was clean, air-conditioned; the dogs were well fed. Their problems start when they leave and, sometimes, before they arrive. Breeders know if a puppy will perform well even at six to eight months of age. There's no way of telling what happens to those who don't show promise. For a very few, like Thetalentedmrripley, the winningest dog in Derby Lane history, there may be breeding fees. But poor-performing dogs are culled, and even fast runners begin to slow down by the time they're five or six. For as many as 10,000 greyhounds a year, retirement may mean adoption and a new life as a pet. But for perhaps twice that number, retirement means isolation, mistreatment, and death.

If greyhounds are among the most victimized breeds, they also elicit great special compassion. Greyhound rescue and adoption groups abound, although the American Kennel Club's Greyhound Rescue somewhat misses the point with its focus on the rescue of AKC greyhounds. AKC greyhounds don't race. There are far fewer of them than racing greyhounds. In 2003, 136 greyhound puppies were registered with the AKC. In 2000, the last year for which I could find numbers, the National Greyhound Association registered 26,464 pups. AKC Greyhound Rescue is like Norfolk Terrier Rescue, Shih-tzu Rescue, or Sussex Spaniel Rescue, very nice but not exactly urgent. Dogs often inspire the desire to do good, and that altruism takes many forms.

GOOD DOGS

> *I could never take dogs for granted. Why are they so devoted to the human race?*
>
> — James Herriot, *Dog Stories*

Since 9/11, service dogs have been lauded repeatedly for their work at Ground Zero, the subject of photo essays and television specials. At the same time, our idea of what a service dog is has expanded. At least mine has. There are service dogs who anticipate their people's epileptic seizures and service dogs who help the handicapped make the bed. Bonnie Dalzell's dogs give blood. In order to give blood, the dogs must not test positive for various chronic illnesses and not have received transfusions. In other words, they have to be in pretty good health themselves, which is no mean achievement for borzoi. And they have to be calm enough to lie on their sides for close to ten minutes. I think it will be a very cold day in hell before George lies still with a needle in him for ten seconds, much less ten minutes, but I wonder sometimes if not sharing him with the world isn't selfish.

Maybe doing good could be George's extracurricular activity. Maybe George doesn't need a hobby like agility or chasing rodents. He is incontrovertibly cute. He's very sweet to people he likes, most of the time, and occasionally to total strangers. There's a woman at the top of the block who gets all excited when she sees George. She coos and pets him, and calls him the mayor of the street. George abides. Surely, there must be a way to share George's healing spirit. In the world of service animals, it really does take all kinds.

Although Rachel McPherson has lived in New York for twenty years and Brooklyn for at least half that time, she still sounds as if she just got off the bus from the Mississippi farm on which she grew up. In 1998, she founded the Good Dog Foundation to assist, train, and place volunteers and their dogs into hospitals, hospices, and geriatric and pediatric facilities. The organization now encompasses some 250 active volunteers and their incredibly varied dogs. One of the first was Niagara, Tracy's first greyhound, who took to therapy work when she got too old to run. Another, a recently deceased Neapolitan Mastiff named Yuffie, was also the alleged author of an advice column called "Ask Yuffie" that ran on the Web site of FIDO, the organization of Prospect Park dog people. Yuffie has recently spoken from the beyond, and her column has become a kind of best-of retrospective site. At the other end of the size spectrum is Rachel's own dog, a papillon named Fidel, who was among the dogs that comforted families of victims who traveled to Ground Zero on ferries in the days following 9/11, when there was no other way in or out of the site.

Who would have thought that papillons, fluffy little creatures with big ears and lambent eyes, could be therapy dogs? Actually, Rachel would; that's why she got one. Attuned, she says, "to the smell of grief and pain," Fidel can remain calm in the embrace of mourners grieving at hysterical pitch. In hospitals, he remains relaxed while patients doing arm exercises lift and lower him as if he were a free weight.

Dogs are trained for therapy work the same way they're trained to do anything else, but these activities don't feel like your standard pet trick. No, therapy dogs exude intimations of higher consciousness, deeper feeling, human compassion.

And that's where I wonder about George. Appealing as he is, he's not that malleable. He doesn't like to sit on anyone's lap too long, let alone a stranger's. He doesn't always want to be petted, even if he knows you. And he's not likely to sit patiently by anyone's side for any length of time. I suspect he could be trained to put all that aside, if we kept at it long enough. I know of one Norfolk who works in hospitals. But I can't quite see George doing it yet, nor me, for that matter. Neither of us has the equanimity for it. Someday, when I have time and George has calmed down, whatever that means, we'll take classes together. Then we'll roam far and wide, spreading George's personal touch. Until then George is my therapy dog, and my wife's and son's. All dogs are therapy dogs to the people who care for them. The distance between family pet and family therapy dog is insignificant.

6. breed poetics

FAMILY VALUES

Dogs, as we know, originated from a common ancestor, and, were all the dogs in the world to be released and the guiding hand of man removed, I presume after a certain number of years the original ancestor would again appear, and what a dreadful creature he was, and would be . . .

— Foreword to *The American Kennel Club Blue Book of Dogs*, 1938 edition

King Carlos II of Spain (1661–1700) was nothing if not well born. The last Hapsburg emperor was a lineal descendant of Queen Juana the Mad of Castille (1479–1555), who earned her nickname by way of irrational rages and other behavioral problems of the rich. On the assumption that the best way to keep the Hapsburg bloodline strong was to keep it in the family, Juana's descendants married one another, cousins to nieces to nephews and so forth. When I say Carlos was a lineal descendant, I mean a very straight line. Besides Juana, twenty-two other ancestors of Carlos exhibited some form of madness. He was epileptic, feeble-minded, and walked with difficulty. He suffered from suppurating ulcers and diseased bones and teeth. His Hapsburg jaw was so prognathous that he couldn't chew, his tongue so large he had trouble speaking. He spent most of his adult life trying unsuccessfully to beget an heir.

On paper, Carlos's pedigree looks a bit like a top show dog's. A lot of the same names pop up again and again. Carlos's parents, for instance, were uncle and niece, so Carlos's mother was also his cousin. Same with dogs; the more you look at the way dogs' pedigree bloodlines develop, the more it seems that all dogs in a breed are cousins. Genetic lines double back and reinforce themselves. When humans mate with close relatives, it's incest; when dogs do it, it's called line breeding.

Without line breeding, there would be

no breed standards, because only by strictly controlling genetic input can breeders manipulate the appearance of dogs to the degree required by a written breed standard. Well-spaced, evenly colored spots on a Dalmatian, the corkscrew coil of a pug's tail, the pale eyes of a Catahoula leopard dog do not happen by accident.

Human line breeding leads pretty quickly to messed-up humans. In fairness, it must be said that its practitioners usually don't have much in the way of a breeding plan. Canine line breeding, on the other hand, implemented by people who know what they're doing, can result in beautiful dogs.

George has one grandparent each from two notable British kennels, Nanphan and Jaeva, but I don't know if there's any line breeding in his pedigree. I figure the odds are good, though, given the highly documented and narrow ancestry of his kind, especially since the Great Schism of 1979.

The Great Schism was not some obscure sectarian repercussion from Vatican II involving Mel Gibson's father. It was the culmination of efforts by the drop-eared faction of the Norwich Terrier Club to distinguish their dogs from their prick-eared co-breed members. Susan Ely says that in the dark days before the Norfolk breakaway, Norwich people had to identify themselves to one another by asking "Are you prick or drop?" As a result of the schism, I have the assurance of knowing that George is descended from two other cute, shaggy, reddish-brown dogs with drop ears and that he is not the random issue of a prick and a drop. Not to suggest that George is the product of an incestuous home or that beneath his luxuriant coat genetic time bombs are ticking away, but it seems inevitable that some cousins or something are in there.

Line breeding doesn't necessarily lead to disaster, at least not right away. Kay McKinstry tells me she has bred grandparent to grandchild with no ill effects. Several other breeders I asked thought that was acceptable. It creeps me out, but to them it's fine. It's also as good an illustration as you'll find of the difference between breeding for conformity to a standard and breeding for working ability.

Breeding to a standard is a relatively recent phenomenon. Until the mid-nineteenth century, there were no recorded breed standards and no clear template how a specific type of dog should look. Breeders have always kept meticulous records, but the goals always seem to have been working ability and temperament.

That changed when, for the first time, a substantial number of people, the strapping new middle class, could afford to keep dogs as pets, a luxury previously enjoyed only by the wealthy. The first purebred dogs were tangible symbols of well-being, the BMWs of their day. Like all status symbols, their prestige did not rest on beauty alone.

By definition, arriviste strivers have no lineage to speak of. But a pedigree dog does, and in the spirit of making sure their dogs looked as special as they presumably were, Victorians began the practice of selective breeding to heighten specific physical characteristics, functional or not. A new doggie elite came into being, its bona fides based on parentage and looks, rather than functional ability. My dog is better than your dog, not because it's better at herding sheep or catching mice, but because it's got a longer neck or a tail that curls just so. Stud books and registries keep track of which dogs sired and which dams begat which dogs and bitches. Even today these terms are so quaint that, spoken aloud, as in "That Coco's such a beautiful bitch," they elicit a smirk from all but the most entrenched fanciers.

What does a century and a half of breeding to strict type teach us? Simply that there is a price to pay. Irish setters, a popular breed in the 1950s, are as lustrously red-coated as they ever were, but they have become, as a veterinarian named Michael W. Fox once said, "so dumb they get lost on the end of their leash." Turns out the gene that controls lustrous red coats controls other stuff too. And the principle holds for humans. Even overlooking an extreme case like poor King Carlos, look at what generations of breeding among the best families in Britain have produced: the royals.

If all this sounds like an extension of the class system to another species, it is — so it's not surprising that the serious business of pedigree, stud registries, and show began in England. The first recorded multiple-breed show was held in Newcastle-Upon-Tyne in 1859. (The first single-breed show — all schipperkes — was in 1690 in Belgium, but that's another story.) Between 1867 and 1886, five editions of *The Dogs of the British Islands*, books that set breed standards that are more or less intact in Britain today, were published. At the same time, dog portraiture, another expression of luxury, was growing in popularity. These detailed renderings of breeds helped to define them. The rise of the purebred dog has as much to do with publishing and painting, nineteenth-century versions of what we'd now call branding, as with the animals themselves.

Written breed standards are key to the fancy, for they are the opponents against which all the dogs compete. The strangely hermetic atmosphere at a dog show is due to the fact that, unlike just about any other competitive activity you can name, the principals in the contest — the dogs — are not competing against one another. Nor are they performing a task that can be objectively measured, like a round of golf or a pole vault. Between the dogs, there is no interplay or upmanship or strategy (though the same cannot be said for the people involved). In a dog show, theoretically at least, the only competition that matters is the one going on inside the judge's head. That contest pits each individual dog against the Platonic ideal of its breed, as enshrined in the written standard. Who says philosophy has no relevance in the modern world?

Written breed standards are mighty strange documents. They seek to convey the essential nature of a particular breed along with the physical necessities. As expressions of what one wants in a particular kind of dog, they do fine. But as lodestars for breeding, they leave much to be desired. Breed descriptions are created and approved by individual breed clubs. In other words, they are written by enthusiasts, admirers, fans, not necessarily experts. The result is a yeasty amalgam of fustian and fact, with the fustian usually overriding. Having toiled through seventy-five years' worth of AKC guides, I've concluded that the American Kennel Club needs to create a salary line for an editor, and pronto.

Looking for a quality Afghan? Naturally, you want one with a "proudly carried head, eyes gazing into the distance as if in memory of age past." (This overcooked language first appeared in the 1949 AKC breed guide, and is still there today.) A greyhound is "swift as a ray of light; graceful as a swallow; and wise as a Solomon." That wise? It's also "a dog that needs no fanfare to herald his approach, no panoply to keep him in the public eye," a description that any number of greyhound rescue groups would dispute. American foxhounds have "voices like the bells of Moscow." "As a sagacious, intelligent house pet and companion, no breed is superior" to your Manchester terrier, so get your act together. Scottish terriers have a "philosophical nature" and are not only "alert and spirited but also stable and steady-going," and in addition "determined and thoughtful."

I am not worthy.

In addition to being overblown, breed standards are often vague. "The poodle has about him an air of distinction and dignity peculiar to himself." Illuminating, no? You could say the same about an earthworm.

Other cultures describe their dogs differently. The Chinese standard for the shar-pei, a loose-skinned, rough-coated breed that was a fad in the 1970s, is poetic and calls for, among other traits, a head like a melon, ears like clamshells, feet like garlic, toenails like iron, a face like a grandmother, a neck like a water buffalo, and an anus that faces the sky.

American breed standards are more aspirational than descriptive. In *The Intelligence of Dogs*, Stanley Coren surmised that 90 percent of AKC breed standards include intelligence as a distinct characteristic. That was an exaggeration. In the current nineteenth edition, the percentage is closer to 80. Fifty-eight AKC breeds are said to have "intelligent expressions," including dogs as various as the Saint Bernard and affenpinscher. Of the 150 AKC breeds, 98 are "intelligent," 76 are "alert," 37 are "dignified," 17 are "elegant," 7 are "noble," and 5 are "aristocratic."

With due respect to the dogs and to the AKC, those words don't describe the dogs; they describe the way we like to think about them. When we speak about the rescue dogs at Ground Zero, for example, we talk about their sacrifice and courage. But as Anne Culver, director of Disaster Services at the Humane Society, told me: "To the rescue dogs, the work is the game they're playing. They're pleasing their human. There's no sense of a tragic dimension." That doesn't make them less admirable or their work less impressive; it makes them dogs.

Setting aside the moral issues that lurk around the pedigree world, I find the dogs mesmerizing, and I believe that responsible breeders are aware of the pitfalls of their work. The term "responsible breeders" is used so frequently by dog people that it deserves its own abbreviation. All the breeders I've talked to are RBs. Their dogs are of high quality, live well, and are sold only after extensive vetting of prospective buyers. How can you tell if a breeder is legit? If a breeder is doing really well, there's probably something ugly going on. RBs do it for love, obsession, whatever. They are lucky if they can break even; most lose money. The only breeders who make a substantial profit off their dogs are running puppy mills, overbreeding their dogs without regard to the health of the individuals. They are the seamy underbelly of the pet business. Still, most pet shop/ puppy mill dogs come with AKC papers, along with their deviated septums and dysplastic hips.

BREED RAPTURE

> i heard a
> couple of fleas
> talking the other
> day says one come
> to lunch with
> me I can lead you
> to a pedigreed
> dog says the
> other one
> i do not care
> what a dog's
> pedigree may be

Don Marquis, *Archy and Mehitabel*

Trying to figure out why people fall for one breed or another is like figuring out why people fall in love. You can find leading indicators, but ultimately there's no accounting for taste. I know someone who grew up with springer spaniels and has continued with them into adulthood, an unbroken succession of springer spaniels all her life. My friend Sam's aunt always had a male wirehaired fox terrier named Lucky; when one Lucky's luck ran out, another Lucky took his place. "You'd go away for a few years, return for a visit and Lucky's still there, same as ever, like Dorian Gray," Sam says. This Wandering Jew–like continuity — the dog that will not die — gives me the willies, but maybe if you always know your dog is going to be Lucky, you'll be less likely to confuse your dog's name with those of your spouse or kids. It's a sounder reason for breed devotion than many I've heard, including the opinion of one acquaintance who declares golden retrievers to be the breed of choice because they will sit on your feet.

Because I had very little to do with our choice of dog, I was unprepared for the torrent of advice, warning, and general enthusiasm that greeted me as I appeared in the nabe with George.

"Whoa, terriers! Really a handful, I bet"

is a sample of the spontaneous bonhomie I have endured.

"A big dog in a small package!" is another.

Has there ever been a small dog in a big package? And who knew dog owners were so gaga over their particular dogs? Or that terrier people would be so terrierlike? I mean, they marvel over things that are just *not so damn marvelous,* perfect strangers rolling their eyes with riotous pooch tales, creating a blockage in the pedestrian flow of my shopping street, while my jaw aches from oversmiling so the other dog owners know I like their dogs too, and respect them to boot. Why do dog lovers have to express their enthusiasm so, well, doggedly?

Some people have great rapport with the breeds they pick. After growing up with exuberant, barky rough collies, Fran Wright was drawn to the quiet solemnity of the borzoi, so at the age of twenty-one, she took out a loan to buy one. She's had borzoi ever since.

Robert Seitz, the breeder I met on the flight home from Crufts, fell for the animal formerly known as the Russian wolfhound on the stage. Born in Russia, Robert emigrated to these shores as a child and grew up in the bosom of showbiz. Before he was out of his teens, he had performed with Horace Heidt and His Musical Knights, with Major Bowes, and alongside a young Theresa Brewer in an act called Uncle Jules' Kiddie Show in Toledo, Ohio. He recalls a production number from *The Great Ziegfeld* in which a half dozen borzoi appeared. "I fell in love with them, and years later, when I had the chance to get this champion bitch, I did." That was in the 1950s and he's still at it. His Ramadi Kennel shares dogs with the Manitias Kennel in Devon, England.

Not all breeders are committed to one breed, but most are. And when a breeder branches out, it's usually into a similar breed. Barbara Miller started with soft-coated wheaten terriers, for instance. Sometimes there's another connection, like the Russian terrier Robert Seitz acquired on one of his frequent trips to what he still refers to as Mother Russia.

The lack of that singular focus should've been the tipoff a couple of years ago, when the Toy Munchkin scandal rocked the Pomeranian world, by which I do not mean folks who live in Pomerania. You may remember them from their appearances on *Animal Planet* and Leeza Gibbons's morning show: four- to five-pound dogs with lion cuts, big manes, and tiny shaved butts. Said to be bred by and for royalty (which royalty?), neutered pups (so no one else could start a breeding program) were being sold for five thousand a pop. Turns out they were actually undersized and not very healthy poms. The only breeder implicated in the mess was one Dawn Roller, whose previous breeding experience had been with Neapolitan mastiffs. You'd think someone would've twigged how weird that was. Dawn Roller, by the way, is now on the banned breeder list of the American Neapolitan Mastiff Association.

Robert Seitz, like many dog lovers, has idiosyncratic ways of interpreting his dogs' behavior. By way of illustrating the extraordinary attachment borzoi form with their people, he told me that while he was away at Crufts for four days, his beloved bitch peed on and around his bed every day, sometimes twice. I wondered if that isn't perhaps more loyalty than I want George to feel on my behalf.

"Nothing will turn a man's home into a castle more quickly and effectively than a dachshund," Queen Victoria said, and of all small breeds, none has a bigger identification with the big-dog-small-package conceit than the famously loyal, possessive, and feisty weiner dog. And no breed has more thoroughly committed owners. It is not because they're particularly easy to live with, according to Ruth Remington, a recent Miami transplant who is the driving force behind the South Beach Dachshund Fest, now in its second year. She describes her dachs, Audrey Hepburn, as "willful and stubborn," a maker of many nonnegotiable demands. "When we lived in Manhattan, Audrey hated Second Avenue, so we had to walk her on First." She also took a long time to house-train, which is par for the breed, Ruth says. "They just don't seem to get it." On the other hand, "Audrey knows how to work a room."

Dachshunds are consistently among the most popular breeds in the country, and dachshund people are extremely inventive in finding extraordinary ways to express their affection for them. These were the thoughts that ran through my mind as I approached Washington Square Park in Greenwich Village for the twelfth annual Dachshund Fiesta in April 2003. It was bright and sunny, a good day for dachshunds and the people who love them. These particular people love their dachshunds enough to dress them in tutus, Mets uniforms, sun hats, dresses, tuxedos, and strap-on styrene hot dog buns with a plastic mustard squiggle on the top. A couple pushed an old-fashioned perambulator so their dachshund, who was recovering from surgery, could be there. A man wearing black leather chaps held his dachs on a studded leash. The emotional high point of the event was the group sing-along of the Dachshund Song ("Most kinds of dogs seem to either/ Have shapes or proportions all wrong;/ They're only one way or the other,/ But dachshunds are both short and long").

It was during the singing that I noticed my internist.

He was there with his wife and their venerable dachshund, Rosie. She was not in costume, which I found inchoately reassuring. On the other hand, my doctor knew all three verses so well he didn't need one of the lyric sheets that were circulating. I wondered if I would mention this sighting when I went in for my physical and decided against. At least he wasn't wearing lederhosen, which is more than I could say for some of the participants.

As peculiar as the Dachshund Fiesta seemed to me, it's business as usual to

April Scott, founder and proprietor of Dachshund Delights, the first (though no longer the only) all-dachshund pet supply house. When I spoke to her, she was off to Montana for the Great Falls Dachshund Days. April flies to one such event or other every couple of weeks from her home in Garrettsville, Ohio. These are not AKC-registered contests. They are neither conformation nor obedience nor agility contests (agile dachshunds?), and they are certainly not earth-dog competitions, where dachshunds on the hunt are anything but cute. These events rarely have official sanctions, although Ruth Remington did get the mayor of Miami to officially proclaim a South Beach Dachshund Day. Some, like the Great Falls event, raise money for charity. But mostly they are opportunities for dachshund people to get together and goof on their dogs.

Scott started Dachshund Delights in 1991 when she heard about an all-Scottie dog business in Kentucky. In terms of growth potential, Scotties have advantages over dachshunds, even though there are far more dachshunds than Scotties (about 40,000 dachs registrations a year compared to about 3,500 Scotties). Merchandise with Scottie dogs on them is "popular with people of Scottish heritage and with people who are named Scott," Ms. Scott says. You don't need to love dogs to love Scotties, apparently, if your name is Scott.

But this particular Ms. Scott grew up with dachshunds and she has connected with a committed clientele. Dachshunds, let's not forget, have some special issues. The sausage shape means they can slip out of standard harnesses easily, which is why the Hug-A-Dog Harness "transfers most of the pressure from the neck to the chest area . . . much better for a doxie's sensitive back." Send in the measurements and you can get one to your specifications. (Hug-A-Dogs have been made to fit a rabbit and a great Dane.) The Potty House, a little clear plastic enclosure like a miniature greenhouse, offers a little dry ground to dachshunds, especially long-haired ones, who don't like to get their undercarriages wet in rainy weather.

This kind of popularity can backfire. A Miller Lite Beer commercial in the early 1990s, which featured racing dachshunds, became so popular that Miller began sponsoring such races at greyhound tracks. In 1995 the Dachshund Club of America issued a statement deploring the practice, fearing the races would encourage "the breeding of dogs for that purpose rather than as examples of the breed standard as recognized by the American Kennel Club."

Dachshund people may be the most visible community in the Dog World, but they're not the largest. In the days when my exposure to dog culture was limited to Westminster on the tube, I assumed that the dog show world was a sort of lunatic fringe that achieves a yearly apotheosis at the Garden. I've since learned that even if they are lunatics, their numbers make them more than a fringe. They are a whole garment. Almost 2 million dogs were entered in AKC-sanctioned dog shows in 2003. That figure does not include the dogs entered in any of the 13,379 agility trials, 2,390 obedience events, 338 tracking events, and 3,527 other performance events sponsored by the AKC that year. During the single week from April 30 to May 6, there were 308 separate all-breed and specialty dog shows. And that figure does not include the dog events sponsored by organizations other than the AKC, including many hunting and racing clubs as well as alternative dog registries like the American Rare Breed Association, the United Kennel Club, and the American Treeing Feist Association.

Although there are far more performance events than dog shows, dog shows have more participants. I was surprised to learn this, because nothing seems more esoteric and peculiar to me than a bunch of dogs walking in a circle. But hundreds and hundreds of thousands of dog people disagree. If you'd like a snapshot of the Dog World sensibility, check out the parking area of a dog show, where vile punnage runs amok: SHNAUZ-R, KAY-9, APSONUT, DOBEE, ARFARF, and BITCH are some of my favorites. I've admired the austere simplicity of NORFOLK, which I've seen in several state colors. You know, come to think of it, maybe the BITCH plate has nothing to do with dogs.

FOOTHILLS OF THE FANCY

Show dogs and their handlers remind me of Brooke Shields and her mother: an incredibly disheveled person tethered to an impeccably groomed animal.

— Margo Kaufman

237

I drove to Ringwood State Park in northern New Jersey on a brisk Friday because I wanted to see who in Greater New York had the time to take a whole Friday off to attend the Greater New York Borzoi Specialty. The answer is, enough people to show 104 borzoi and use over fifty cars to get them all there. Many of the vehicles were bulky SUVs and RVs, which made parking difficult. Their drivers tend to space them as widely as possible; several times I'd thought I found a spot, only to edge around one of the behemoths to find myself facing a borzoi grooming station or a picnic.

Fran Wright, then secretary of the Greater New York Borzoi Club, had been there since six-thirty in the morning, putting up canopies, arranging the chairs and tables and open-sided tents where the judges preside. I arrived late, around noon — New Jersey always turns out to be bigger than I think it's going to be — when the dogs on show were the "beloved friend class," meaning dogs who used to compete and are now retired, though I think some of them were just older dogs belonging to club members, not show animals at all. I wondered briefly what it would mean for George to retire. How would his days be different from what they are now? Would he understand that he was retired?

It was certainly lovely to see these imposing, elegant dogs standing in lines by the edge of a still lake that reflected a lowering sky. They are tall and slim, with curving backs and long, narrow heads. They look Brahmin, like John Kerry without the bouffant.

Small, local dog shows like these are the real heart of the fancy. Few of the dogs you see at them go on to be campaigned as serious show dogs. But the dogs who end up on television start in shows like these. And this is also where many junior handlers start out, those impossibly clean-cut–looking nerdlingers who have only a moment in the spotlight at the big shows. Most of the handlers here are the owners of the dogs, which to hard-core dog fanciers is the real point of the exercise.

Fran Wright says, "A professional handler can make any dog look good. That's their job. But if you take your own dog that you've trained yourself and make him do what you want, that's a good dog." Kay McKinstry concurs: "There's a fabulous feeling to finishing a dog yourself. The fun is being there, not just having your name on a dog that someone else trains and shows."

The borzoi show was a national specialty, which means that the awards and points won there count toward the dogs' official standings in the fancy. The Norfolk event I'd attended earlier was a match show, not a specialty, which is lower down the competitive scale. Match shows don't affect AKC standing, so many of the dogs entered are pets, not really show dogs. The mood was very relaxed. For me, the opportunity to see forty-odd Norfolks in one place was worth the trip, even if I did spend most of the day standing around in a field so full of poo that I wondered what they were feeding the dogs, until I realized it was from geese. When the Superbitch Class was called, a woman led her entry into the ring and airily announced, "Now that I've been properly addressed, we can begin."

THE GLORY AND THE BUZZ

A man could create an entire race, a whole new breed based on tits alone — or hips or legs or turned-up noses and pinned-back ears. Look what they've done with dogs.

— T. C. Boyle, *Riven Rock*

The Westminster Kennel Club Dog Show is, as anyone remotely connected with it will tell you repeatedly and at the drop of a hat, the second-oldest sporting event in the nation, superseded only by the Kentucky Derby. It is the only event that has been staged at all four iterations of Madison Square Garden, and it predates the American Kennel Club by seven years. Show and club were founded in 1877 by "sporting gentlemen" who enjoyed socializing in the bar of the Westminster Hotel. Unlike the Kentucky Derby, the dog show's athletic demands are dubious at best, but the two events share something beside antiquity: Both have their origins in the primordial urge of those who've got it to flaunt it, baby, flaunt it.

Back when socialites were more like Edith Wharton and less like the Hilton sisters, Westminster was a highlight of the New York season. Foreign royalty was represented, too. In 1889 the czar's dog competed; the next year a borzoi belonging to the emperor of Germany was entered. Pedigree dogs were immensely popular by this time, but only the truly wealthy could afford to maintain the big kennels where purebreds could be tweaked and refined over generations of controlled breeding.

The competition at Westminster is still the province of those who can afford to get there. Admission is by invitation only and restricted to dogs who have already earned enough points in AKC-sanctioned shows to put a "Ch." for champion before their names. The process of earning that title — campaigning a dog, it's called — is costly. There are entry fees, transportation, lodging, grooming, and veterinary costs. There are handling fees, since most top-ranked dogs in the United States are shown by professional handlers, not their owners. "In the long run, it's cheaper," Richard Reynolds says. "They know how to show your dog and where to show."

There is also advertising to consider. Serious contenders advertise their dogs in the *Canine Chronicle*, *Dog News*, and other organs of the fancy. This is not considered a frill. Advertising is essential to a dog's chances at the big time since, as a bull terrier breeder told me, "If the judges don't know you, you haven't got a chance." In all, campaigning a dog can run $10,000 a month, which is why there are few surprises in the show ring. Not many people come out of the woodwork with that kind of money to spend on a dog.

There are exceptions, of course, such as

the owner of Jack, a mellow and enormous mastiff I met at the 2004 show in the scrum of spectators clogging the aisles around the show rings. Jack's owner (and handler) was a young woman wearing what looked to me like an old-fashioned prom dress. She alternately touched up her makeup and fussed over Jack, who took her adjustments of his enormous, loose mouth and abundant jowls in stride. The girl was talking to herself, to Jack, or to anyone passing by. "I'm so nervous. We've just got here from Arizona," she said, as if she'd just double-parked outside. Jack didn't look nervous. Maybe his part-time gig as a therapy dog had inured him to pressure, or perhaps it was the regional specialty show he'd won en route to the big city. In any case, he looked totally unfazed, sitting patiently in the crush of humanity, receiving pats and smiles and head rubs as his due. It was hard not to rub his head; it was the biggest head I've ever seen. His scrotum was nothing to sniff at, either, unless you were another dog, and even then I would be very, very careful.

During the two days Westminster is in residence at the Garden, the rings and backstage areas are clotted with visitors, dogs, and temporary stalls selling everything from spaniel brooches to designer kibble. Its prime-time evening broadcasts are watched by millions. Despite the fact that Westminster, like any dog show, is all about class, snobbery, and bloodlines — the rich loam from which violent revolutions grow — the atmosphere is startlingly egalitarian. Sure, there's still some of the old guard left: bottle-blonde ladies-who-lunch in their casually elegant daytime wear and sport-coated men in club ties and Weejuns and breed-specific lapel pins. As long as there are dog shows, the loafer tassel industry and the Barbour jacket people have nothing to worry about. But there are also retired gents with white shoes and pastel cardigans, their wives sporting helmet hair sprayed into submission. There are beefy guys who look like UPS men ogling the rotties, young women with pug hats, and even a disaffected existentialist type, thin-lipped like Jeremy Irons, all in black with a carefully trimmed goatee and, subverting the effect of his groovy ensemble, an unconvincing hairpiece, painstakingly directing some young Japanese girls with spiky multihued hair to the French bulldog area. Wandering around, I couldn't help but feel a kinship with this motley crowd. We are the doggers.

Westminster is dismissed by some as too commercial, too crowded, and too common. I've been told that a win at the World Dog Show or the Montgomery all-terrier show carries more prestige than one at Westminster. But never in dispute is the fact that Westminster is the public face of the fancy in this country. It is the one show everyone's heard of, the subject of the hilarious *Best in Show* and briefly a backdrop for *Sex in the City*. For me, the 2004 show was different. For the first time I was a partisan. I was rooting for Coco, the Norfolk. Who else?

My hope had some foundation, too, not like the quixotic dreams of the schipperke crowd. I mean, I'm sure they root-root-root for their dogs every year, but if no one is sure how to pronounce the name, what do you think the chances are of winning something? I wonder, has a schipperke ever won anything at Westminster?

On the morning of Monday, February 9, 2004, gossip columnist Cindy Adams of the *New York Post* intimated that Coco was heavily tipped to win. This was not a hunch. In dog circles, Coco was a rising star, the most successful dog on the circuit over the past year. She'd had already won a couple of BISs (Best in Shows) at Montgomery, the venerable all-terrier show, and the Eukanuba Classic (like the Coke Classic, the Eukanuba is a relative newcomer, created for television and staged the week before Westminster). She's also an English import, and they have always gone down well in New York. Take *Cats*, for instance — please.

That morning I arrive early and head to the backstage area, which is open to the public. Westminster is a "benched" show, which means that the dogs and their handlers and/or owners are on display even when not in the ring, so the hoi polloi can get a closer look at the dogs, ask questions, see about buying a puppy. You can also find here every conceivable dog accessory, toy, and doohickey. Does anybody actually buy those scraggly pewter figurines? Every breed looks like a Giacometti.

The benching area is the best reason to attend Westminster in person — but only if you get there early because, by mid-afternoon, the place feels like rush hour on the subway. The benching area is where the dogs are most impressive from a performing and poise point of view. Most of them are there all day, asleep in crates or sitting atop or beside them, petted, prodded, and peered at from 8 a.m. to 4 p.m. In my four visits, I've never seen a dog fight, or even a bit of unpleasantness between visitor and canine. These dogs are seriously mellow.

In fact, many of them look positively narcotized. Are they in standby mode? Are they reciting their mantras? Here a komondor lolls, eyelids at half-mast, the tendrils of its long corded coat wrapped in tissue like a lady at the beauty parlor — only a glance at his hindquarters makes it clear he ain't no lady. A beefy woman takes the ample head of her impassive Bernese mountain dog in both hands and closes her eyes, like Mr. Spock trying to communicate with that creature everyone thought was a boulder. A man in a snow-white duffle coat navigates the mob with a limp Löwchen tucked delicately in the crook of his arm like a crystal football.

The little dogs appear the most out of it. The shih-tzus looked stoned. (Did you hear about the shih-tzu–bull terrier cross? They call it a bull shih-tz.) A pug sits on its crate, half reclining on one hip like the White Rock Maiden, breathing noisily through its flat nose, eyes glassy. The lights are bright, there's lots of noise, and the crowded aisles surge with humanity.

I know plenty of dog people who would

be repelled by the sight of such primped dogs set out for display in such an unnatural setting, but it's less clear to me how the dogs feel about it. At a small match show that included a category for senior dogs, an owner/handler told me that older dogs love the opportunity to strut their stuff one more time — smell of the greasepaint, roar of the kibble, I suppose.

But now there's no more time to meander. It's getting close to one o'clock. If the fancy is a sport, then I'm assuming a vital role that I would never have dreamed of. I'm a fan, a supporter, maybe even a hooligan in the making. How much difference is there between me and those soccer fans who go ape at matches in Europe? We'll find out.

By 3:10 the crowd around Ring 3 is packed, and the Norfolks aren't due for twenty minutes. Only a few feet away at Ring 5, the papillons seem to be watched only by the handlers' mothers. The sound in the arena, though, is an unrelenting din. Breeds have claques, just like opera singers. All around the place, you hear wild cheering go up every time some pug or Irish setter makes its counterclockwise circle for the judge. (The circle has to be counterclockwise, because dogs walk on the handler's left, and the object of the circle is to show the dog in motion.) In 1849, New York's Astor Place riots erupted between admirers of the Shakespearean actors William Macready and Edwin Forrest. Why shouldn't there be fisticuffs between warring breed enthusiasts? My Chihuahua can lick your schnauzer.

Much of the crowd around Ring 3 looks familiar. There's Judith Felton of ANTA; Nat LaMar, a former breeder and fellow Brooklynite, editor of the latest edition of *The Norfolk Terrier*; Richard Schiller, the Manhattan groomer who specializes in Norfolks, Norwich, and the occasional cairn, and who is known in Norfolk circles worldwide (George is a client, natch); and the wife of the man I met at Montgomery who believes fervently that the earl of Oxford is the true author of the works of Shakespeare, whom he refers to dismissively as "the man from Stratford." Barbara Miller is here, of course, wearing chartreuse and looking intensely at the ring, even though it's full of Cavalier King Charles spaniels. There are lots of the damn things, and the big-haired judge is taking her sweet time judging them. Don't they understand there are Norfolks waiting?

I can't say I feel better for having confessed to such base, petty impatience, and I'd also like to apologize right now to all the Cavalier King Charles spaniel people, but I daresay I wasn't the only one in that crowd who was thinking, Enough already.

Not that they aren't remarkable little animals, real demonstrations of what breeders can do, particularly if their product gets a royal endorsement. These dogs were bred down from big hunting spaniels. Along the way their aggression was replaced by the need to request love and return love. So all they want is to snuggle and be petted and to offer kisses.

How can you respect a dog like that? As any dog book will tell you, dogs, being pack animals (don't stop me if you've heard this), need to establish their station within the pack, like gorillas or *Survivor* contestants. Do I want my pet to be purpose-bred for neediness? I think not.

But I digress. I look around that ring and I see a lot of twitching jaws. To be of the fancy is to specialize, and people who are ready for Norfolks don't like to be crammed together looking at spaniels. At the Montgomery show, I saw a couple of Norfolk acquaintances set up their chairs in front of the designated ring and wait.

Hours later, after the Norfolks had finished, they packed up and left.

Eventually the judge picks the winning spaniels. The photographer tosses the toy and snaps the winner. There is general milling in the ring as we wait for the Norfolk smackdown to commence. I congratulate Judith Felton on the new attention to the breed, and she says, "Well, it's a little worrying. We're all bracing ourselves for the onslaught."

I ask why and she drops her voice and looks at me seriously. "Puppy mill."

Great success on the show circuit is a mixed blessing. Fans of the breed want the recognition and breeders want their dogs to be in demand, but as Kay McKinstry wrote me with some relief after the show, "A BIS win at the Garden is NOT good for any breed." Neither is a hit movie.

Dalmations are beautiful and athletic, but difficult, creatures. Even their most ardent admirers would say they are no walk in the park. They are high-strung, need lots of exercise, and have a high incidence of deafness. None of this mattered to less-than-responsible breeders when the *101 Dalmations* movies created a spike in demand for the dogs, followed by a noticeable increase of Dalmations given up to shelters by overwhelmed owners.

I used to resent the idea that a breeder could interview me and had to accept my application before I could get a dog. But now I know why Judith Felton is dubious about the friend I've mentioned who is interested in getting a Norfolk. I attempt to reassure her. "I don't know him that well, but I can tell you that his giant schnauzer puppy is beautifully cared for," I say.

Judith looks skeptical. "Let the schnauzer grow up and then we'll see." A little later she clears up any ambiguities. "If I don't know you, you're not getting a dog."

Eventually the spaniels clear out and I wait for the ring to fill with little George-esque dogs. Nine are listed in the show guide, but only five appear. Two of them are bred by Barbara Miller, but not Coco, the dog with the buzz.

Once the actual judging starts, I am lost. The five Norfolks in the ring all look great, though naturally not as great as George. But they are all winsome, perky little things, well groomed but not ridiculously so, because the breed standard permits "honorable marks of wear and tear," as if these pampered cuties were just out clearing gophers from the north forty. They certainly seem livelier than the dogs back in the benching area. In fact, one would have to say they are not exactly calm and orderly. Not that they're out of line; they can't be out of line, because the thin leashes around their necks don't allow for much range of motion.

I ask Nat LaMar what he thinks of the dogs. Without averting his eyes from the ring, he says, "Look at the eye contact Beth has with her." He's talking about Beth Sweigert, the handler who'd taken Coco to the best in show only the week before at Eukanuba. Sure enough, dog and handler are staring deep into each other's eyes. BFD, I think. George does that, too, especially if he sees me reach into the treat pocket.

Coco takes best in breed, as expected. I ask Nat if he thought she'd been the clear winner. "Absolutely," he says. "You could just see, it was her moment, she was ready for it."

I head home, exhausted both by the excitement and the endless standing around. Time to get ready for the evening's entertainment. The hoi polloi are cleared from the Garden floor and the ring is given over to the evening telecast, where the best of group in three of the seven categories will be selected. Tomorrow night's broadcast will pick the rest of the remaining groups and best in show. Coco's got to take best of group to advance. I'm laying in quantities of beer and dip.

THE INANITY, OH, THE INANITY

"Good Golly, Miss Molly."

— Westminster television commentary about dog named Molly, 2004

Watching Westminster on TV is a completely different experience from being there. In person, everybody's speaking the same language. Even though it's desperately crowded and bulging with commercialism, the show has the intimacy of a cult event. The televised evenings, by contrast, play like a desperate act of salesmanship coupled with the looniest commentary in American sports broadcasting — and by the way, did you know that Westminster is the second-oldest sporting event in the United States?

Westminster has been shown on television since 1948, but only in the last ten years or so has it become the extravaganza it now is, three–four hours of prime time for two nights and an obvious vehicle for the advertising of dog foods, dog medicines, doghouses — and dogs themselves. This is the occasion for the American Kennel Club to get its essential message out, which is that all dogs are good dogs — if they are purebreds registered with the American Kennel Club.

My wife has a theory about the Westminster commentators; she believes they start drinking at the beginning of each show and continue to drink, slowly but steadily, over the entirety of each evening's broadcast until their coherence shrivels entirely, replaced by nothing but ranting praise for every dog who has ever walked the earth or, rather, every *purebred* dog. How else can we explain why the Westminster Dog Show is accompanied by the most banal, irrelevant, and downright dumb-ass chatter to grace any sporting event ever? To wit:

"Today Dalmatians remain the mascots of many firehouses." They do?

A miniature poodle with one of those Ru-Paul hairdos minces by. Commentator announces, apropos of nothing at all: "This is the new hot dog." His compadre joins in the fun: "Hot dog! Hey, I like that!"

They reminisce, to nauseating effect, about "a wonderful golden who changed my life, name of Dakota" and "the one that touched my heart, Casey." Fortunately, moments like these are brief, because of the constant excitement, such as the unexpected revelation that "Bill Cosby is a good dog man."

A blessed moment of dead air occurs, and you can just enjoy looking at the dogs, then one of them opens his yap again, intoning "These are wonderful dogs, wonderful dogs. . . ."

A colleague takes up the torch. "Look how the audience lights up for these dogs!"

Some of this relentless triviality may be due to the fact that of the three who share duties, only David Frei knows much about dogs. Charlsie Cantey is a horse-racing analyst and Mark McEwan is a chatty general interest guy. But Frei's remarks are fully as overheated and vacant as those of his compatriots.

The effusiveness has taken a new turn with the breathless tributes to service dogs that have become de rigueur since 9/11. Charlsie Cantey refers to them as "dogs who give back," which is only slightly less wacky than David Frei's salute to therapy dogs during the 2002 show, in which he lauded them for "providing counseling" to families of 9/11 victims.

There are two things wrong with the way Westminster is presented:

1. *The hard sell of the pedigree ideal:* The American Kennel Club and the Westminster Kennel Club and associates want you not merely to buy a dog, but to buy a purebred dog, that is to say, one with pedigree papers from the AKC. "With a purebred," Frei says, "you know what you're getting," although he knows, as anyone involved with the AKC knows, that registration papers imply no guarantees at all about the health or soundness of a dog.

2. *The refusal to admit that a dog show is not a horse race:* It's decorous. Dogs walk in a circle. A human strolls around them in no great hurry. Male dogs are poked. Teeth are inspected. There is primping. The judge observes, ponders, chooses. Kiss, cry, liver bit, applause. White-knuckled excitement it is not.

But television has its own demands, and one of them seems to be that a sporting event is the same as a sport. This is like saying that if someone is wearing a sport coat, he is an athlete. So every minute or so, David Frei refers to what we're watching as a sport and the dogs standing in lines as athletes.

Frei has been doing this for a long time, and his protestations reached a rare pitch of lunacy in 2002, when one of his copresenters was Joe Garagiola, imported presumably to bring an earthy touch to the proceedings. As a former jock himself, he wondered aloud why Westminster isn't really what it looks like, a beauty pageant. "It's not a beauty pageant because there are definitions for what the dogs have to have," Frei said gnomically, but Garagiola kept trying to put it in terms we could understand. "Which dog is the Diamondbacks? Which one's the Rams?" Frei changed the subject.

The more they call it a sport, the more you know it ain't. That is, in fact, why dog shows are called conformation shows everywhere but on TV; the object is for the dogs to conform, not perform.

The morning after Josh the Newfie won — or, rather, Coco lost — I went up to the Long Meadow with George and ran into my friend Sam. I began lamenting Coco's bad luck, insisting that we wuz robbed and that it was the biggest sports scandal since the 1919 Black Sox. "You can't put a terrier up against a big dog like that and expect to win," Sam stated flatly. Then he admitted to a feeling we shared. "I felt about the best in show the way I feel about the Democratic candidates. I don't care who it is, so long as he can beat the peke."

DOG PEOPLE AND DOG PEOPLE

Canis familiaris is no different from paint or words — a marvelous medium for self-expression.

— Amy Fernandez,
Dog Breeding as a Fine Art

After the Norfolks were done showing back at Crufts, I asked Barbara Miller to explain why the one who'd won best in breed dog was, as she'd pointed out well before the judge did, the only and obvious choice. She started to reply, then stopped and fixed me with a stern look. "Do you understand a dog? Do you really understand what a dog is?" she asked.

My inner smart-ass wanted to say something clever, like "four legs, wet nose, man's best friend?" but I knew Barbara would not find this funny. Barbara takes

259

dogs very seriously. She didn't even find *Best in Show* funny. This opinion, by the way, is shared by many of the fancy. Isn't that amazing?

Barbara's understanding of, and devotion to, Norfolks has brought her awards, respect, and an endless waiting list for her dogs, which tend to be hale and healthy as well as good-looking. There is also no one with whom I'd rather watch a dog show, and not merely because her sense of humor proves that while you can take a person out of Brooklyn, you can't reverse the process. I admit that I'm not exactly objective in my estimation of her, since one of George's not-too-remote ancestors came from her kennel, which, as far as I'm concerned, makes Barbara and me practically cousins.

All the RBs I've met care deeply about dogs, and this energy has maintained distinctive breeds and created new ones. Dogs would not be as diverse, strong, or beautiful if it were not for them. Of course, they wouldn't have medical problems that result from overbreeding, either. And without breeders, we wouldn't have designer crossbreeds like the Labradoodle.

I'd assumed this was breeding lunacy at its most arbitrary, but the truth is that

Labradoodles were developed by Australian breeders looking for a dog who had the service-ready disposition of a Labrador and the nonallergenic coat of a poodle. According to local Labradoodle people (repeat three times fast), a Labradoodle born of two true-breeding Labradoodles is pricier than the issue of a plain-vanilla Lab and poodle.

It's hard to say if any similar functionality informs the peekapoo, schnoodle, or cockapoo, but the Labrahuahua is most certainly a breed with a plan, as Desmond Morris observes in *Dogs*: "This breed was deliberately created by mating a male Chihuahua (standing on two large bags of dog biscuits!) to a female Labrador, in order to produce a smaller-size, placid and helpful hearing dog, to be of assistance to deaf people."

Most breeders, of course, are not trying to create something new. In some cases, in fact, they are trying to re-create something old, like the folks at Good Time Bostonettes, a kennel dedicated to the resurrection of the Olde Boston Bulldogge [*sic*], an antecedent of the Boston terrier but a little bigger, not necessarily black and white, and not much seen for the past century.

I suppose it is a creative impulse to re-create a historic breed, like wanting to restore an Avanti, only with living tissue. But to the breeder, the Olde Boston Bulldogge rights a historic wrong wrought by none other than the fancy itself:

"The knowledge of the dogs is found in many places," the breeder writes. "The truth is found in the dogs themselves. I do not sanction the AKC. They have diminished the gene pool for dogs and have duplicated the effect of unintelligent inbreeding, causing congenital defects such as breathing difficulty, difficulty whelping (often having to have a caesarean section), prominent eyes prone to injury, etc."

The Olde Boston is only one of a raft of niche bulldogs currently in development, such as the Dorset Old Thyme Bulldogge, the Alphalfa Blueblood Bulldog, the Olde English Bulldogge, the Catahoula Bulldog, the Victorian Bulldog, the Mallorquin Bulldog (Ca de Bou in the original Catalan), and the Buldogue Campiero. Some of these are attempts to revive defunct breeds, others the creations of stylin' breeders.

If we look past the extraordinary multiplicity of ways these folks have found to spell "bulldog," we see a whole lot of marginally different, but essentially similar, animals, and the question just begs to be asked: *Don't these breeders have anything better to do with their time?*

No breed seems to have been more subject to the whims of human design than the poor bulldog. It was originally developed in England for the bloody sports of bull- and bear-baiting, which involve a dog clamping its jaws onto the larger animal's nose, ears, or tongue and hanging on as the enraged beast tries to shake it off. To facilitate their gruesome work, bulldogs were bred with compact bodies for dodging bull horns, strong jaws for gripping, and flattened faces with noses recessed behind the jawline, so the dogs could breathe without letting go.

In 1835, bull-baiting became illegal, and bulldogs were out of work. Since then, they have become companion and show dogs, slower and gentler than their forbears, and even more exaggerated in appearance. Today's bulldogs have difficulties coupling, whelping, sleeping, breathing, and walking. Bitches cannot give birth without caesarians, because their hips are too narrow for their broad-headed pups. French bulldogs, whose je ne sais quoi made them popular among nineteenth-century Parisian prostitutes, have flatulence issues.

I wonder if any nouveau bulldogs will avoid these problems or even the lesser ones that beset Winston, the bulldog with separation anxiety. As if his psychological scars weren't enough, Winston suffers as well from skin problems, sinus allergies, and shortness of breath. He needs to be professionally bathed with special unguents and then painstakingly dried. Otherwise, mold grows in his wattles. Fortunately, he is much adored by an owner who appreciates his laid-back style. To her, Winston is "an ottoman that poops and loves me."

I asked Barbara Miller why she put so much time and energy into her dogs, and she gave me a one-word answer: "Ego." But I suspect there's some dog love in there, too. Barbara believes that every litter she breeds is supposed to improve on the previous one. She recalls with particular pride an AKC judge telling her that she had put her mark on her breed.

Not that a skilled trainer can't bring that side out.

Susan Ely's Pinchbeck Norfolks have won every conceivable award for their earth-dog prowess. When one of them competed in the show ring at the Montgomery all-terrier show, I saw her turn away as her dog entered, so distasteful did she find the ritual. I asked her why she bothered showing dogs if she had so little respect for the process. She said, "To show that my dogs can do what they're meant to do and also measure up to the written standard." That damn written standard is the Grail.

The mission of the American Kennel Club is solely to:

- Maintain a registry for purebred dogs and preserve its integrity.
- Sanction dog events that promote interest in, and sustain the process of, breeding for type and function of purebred dogs.
- Take whatever action necessary to protect and assure the continuation of the sport of purebred dogs.

Close textual analysis reveals that there is nothing there about "health." Andrew Rowan of the Humane Society told me that the top Doberman stud dog of the 1980s was hemophiliac and that this was known in the Doberman community. Fran Wright, the borzoi breeder, explained to me that if a borzoi is born with a weak heart that requires medication, that is considered not a problem but a *condition*, a function of being born in accordance with the standard — the price of beauty. Both Fran and Robert Seitz mentioned a breeder who, both said, was solely responsible for the numerous back, hip, and heart problems American borzoi have today. This breeder apparently began with four dogs and has never brought in any outcrosses. I asked why the breeder had never been brought to justice, and both said it was because of her influence at the AKC.

Virtually every person I spoke to in the fancy feels the playing field is anything but level. Many judges are also breeders, and vice versa. Most dogs in the upper reaches of the American fancy are shown by professionals, and they bring their own contacts into the ring. At the same time, there's usually no sure way to tell how much cosmetic buttressing a dog has received until something goes wrong. Richard Reynolds, the breeder and judge, told me he's seen handlers touch up the markings on their dogs with felt-tip pens. Another judge told me that most airedales in the show ring are the same color because they're all wearing the same powder. Problems like this are silly but harmless. The health issues that arise in the pursuit of "typier" dogs are anything but.

In 1940 and '41, a cocker spaniel named My Own Brucie won two consecutive best in shows at Westminster, and cocker spaniels quickly became one of the most popular dogs in America. As the breed became more popular, its appearance changed, since breeders exaggerated the qualities they believed accounted for the dogs' appeal. By 1954, the next time a cocker won best in show, the champion had a stubbier nose, a longer coat, and bigger eyes than the 1941 model.

In the American Kennel Club *Blue Book of Dogs*, 1938 edition, the Pekinese don't look at all like Pekinese today. They have longer legs, more developed muzzles, and less hair. They look more like Tibetan spaniels, from which they are believed to have developed. Danny, the Peke who won best in show at Crufts in 2003, caused a great stir when he turned out to have had plastic surgery. Les, the Peke who won best of the Toy Group at Westminster in 2004, was minuscule, flat-faced, and bug-eyed. His slow, rolling gait is very distinctive of the breed; it looks extremely effortful. With due respect, the dog looked like the Very Hairy Caterpillar.

No offense to the Pekinese crowd, but

Les was at the extreme end of the breed type. The inclination to exaggerate in the name of style is part of human nature: Think tail fins on Cadillacs. But it ain't quite the same as the Platonic ideal.

It would be disingenuous of me, with my well-bred little friend, to decry the American Kennel Club, but it's not out of place to suggest that the organization's resident Platonists have not lived up to their end of the bargain. Breed standards have changed over the years far less than the dogs have. And they've changed in ways that play to the extreme of the standard, the way bodybuilders look in relation to normal people. Hasn't anybody heard of the Aristotelian Golden Mean? Different Greek philosopher, terrific concept. It's also not beyond my station to wish that those in charge took as much interest in the inside of the dog as the outside. That, to me, is the essential difference between the dog people you meet in the fancy and the dog people you meet in the park, and that's why I'm glad I spend more time in the park than at dog shows.

7. george and the heroic ideal

LASSIE AND OTHER DOGS I DON'T LIKE

"If I were a young man, I'd never let them take you from me."

— Jock (Donald Crisp) in
Challenge to Lassie

Balto, the heroic dog who saved an Alaskan town by carrying diphtheria vaccine across the frozen wastes, is memorialized with an imposing statue in Central Park, inspiring generations of New York children to ask what a statue of a doggy is doing there. By the time I learned about Balto, I had seen enough doggy derring-do on television and in movies to be blasé about his achievements.

George has awakened me to the difference between screen dogs and real ones. He may do wonderful things. He might go after someone trying to attack me, for example. And I pity that person. Still, he would have no elevated purpose in doing so. Dogs don't review the situation and then make a decision to be noble and self-sacrificing. Don't look for them to behave along the lines of Sydney Carton going to the guillotine in place of his best friend or Peter Parker giving up his true love to save New Yorkers. They do what they do; forget noble.

Hollywood begs to differ. Historically, dogs are almost as important to the movies as guns or kisses. The reason is the assumed nature of dog person love. It's always believable, usually enviable, and rarely in doubt, which is ideal for commercial pictures. The original Rin Tin Tin, a German shepherd dog rescued from a bombed-out kennel during World War I, is widely credited with saving Warner Bros. Studios from bankruptcy during the 1920s. Impeccably trained by Lee Duncan, the man who had found him in Germany, Rin Tin Tin made twenty-six pictures between 1922 and his death in 1932, including some talkies. Some of them were scripted by Darryl Zanuck, then a young screenwriter. In the 1970s, Paramount released a movie about Rinty's great run called *Won Ton Ton, the Dog Who Saved Hollywood.*

Duncan went on to train the son of Rin Tin Tin and create the dynasty. Rin Tin Tin, Jr., was the first dog to take a commercial flight. After Junior, Rin Tin Tins were given Roman numerals, like SuperBowls. Duncan and Rin Tin Tin III trained more than 5,000 war dogs and handlers during World War II. In the 1950s, several generations and a distinguished outcross or two down the road, Rin Tin Tins II and IV, father and son, were two of the three dogs who played the title role on *The Adventures of Rin Tin Tin* on television. II and IV are also the sources from which the current Rin Tin Tin bloodline flows. Today many of their descendants work in security.

The original Rin Tin Tin movies were serialized tales of valor, with Rinty rescuing kindly fur trappers or ladies inexplicably stuck in the desert. Rin Tin Tin had competitors, notably Strongheart, another German shepherd who played the lead roles in silent versions of *White Fang* and *Call of the Wild.* The dogs in these movies were not exactly companion animals; they were more like avenging angels, defenders of the common weal. Rin Tin Tin was Superman with a tail.

But the hero of the 1950s television show *The Adventures of Rin Tin Tin* was a very different kind of dog. Instead of a warrior, he was a devoted family pet. The show was essentially a Western with a boy and a dog thrown in, the two of them saving the day with a hearty cry of "Yo, Rinty!" If "Yo, Rinty!" sounds suspiciously like the Lone Ranger's "Hiyo, Silver," I think you're onto something, because by this time Rin Tin Tin was no longer top media dog. That distinction was held by Lassie, undoubtedly the most famous movie and TV dog of all time. (Radio, too. The original movie Lassie, real name Pal, provided the barking.)

In *The Politics of Dogs*, Mark Derr recounts a 1989 appearance by Kenneth Marsden, then AKC president, at a hearing in Miami concerning an ordinance to restrict, and ultimately ban, pit bulls or any dogs conforming to the pit bull standard, on the grounds that the breed is inherently dangerous to people. Marsden, seeking to illustrate the point that looks alone are not sufficient to identify a breed, said that he could not definitively say Lassie was a collie without seeing her papers.

For Derr, this is the ultimate idiocy of basing breed identity on pedigree alone, to the exclusion of appearance and function. For me, it's no surprise. I've always had my doubts about Lassie. I suspected that she was played by seventeen dogs spelling each other, or a very clever Chihuahua in a fat suit. Possibly she was yet another virtuoso turn by the remarkable Alec Guinness.

Even during Lassie's halcyon television days, I wasn't much of a fan, and that initial indifference has cooled even more since George arrived. Lassie is responsible for deep feelings of guilt and inadequacy across great swaths of the Dog World. Based on a novel by Eric Knight, a British writer who emigrated to the United States and died in combat in World War II, the movie in which Lassie first appeared on-screen came during the postwar pet explosion and the first flowering of the dog obedience movement. A reviewer of *Lassie Come Home* referred to the eponymous star as "Greer Garson in furs."

Indeed, Lassie was statuesque, long-suffering, and beautiful. She was about as different as could be from the lovers of

Lady and the Tramp, the all-American dog couple of the 1950s. Lassie had neither Lady's femininity nor Tramp's charm. She appeared to have the intellectual heft of Dag Hammarskjöld. She did no tricks, licked no tears away, had no need to play. Her single affectionate gesture was extending a paw. I always found her a cold fish, and now, having revisited much of the Lassie oeuvre, I know there was a deeper reason for my instinctive dislike of the well-coiffed dog diva: Lassie is a pain in the ass.

That said, *Lassie Come Home,* the original, holds up on screen as well as it does in print. The pastel Hollywood versions of England and Scotland are beautiful. The supporting human cast includes stalwarts like Donald Crisp and Edmund Gwenn as well as the incredibly touching young Roddy MacDowell and the petite but already perfectly formed Elizabeth Taylor. They lend believability, grace, and humor to the melodrama. Lassie herself is wonderful to look at, spirited, unswerving in her devotion to her impoverished Yorkshire family, and undaunted by tribulation. Here is a dog — well, theoretically a bitch — whose deeds are inspired by love.

And what deeds they were! In the course

of the movie, Lassie reads road signs; swims the Tweed River; saves a few lives; brings joy into the drear, dead-end lives of Dame May Whitty and Daniel Webster, the elderly couple who save her life; and goes on the road with Edmund Gwenn. She survives gunfire, falls from great heights, starvation, broken bones, and Scottish weather, followed by English weather.

The legend of Lassie is so entrenched that it's sometimes forgotten that her story is fiction. No dog had had a part like this since the 1850s, when New York audiences thrilled to canine heroics in such theatrical melodramas as *The Planter and His Dogs*, *The Fisherman and His Dogs*, and *The Rag Woman and Her Dogs*. In subsequent movies, Lassie got even more extraordinary. Playing her own offspring, she fights Nazis in *Son of Lassie*. In *Hills of Home*, she conquers hydrophobia (the old term for rabies) with the help of Edmund Gwenn (again). In *Courage of Lassie*, she licks amnesia with help of Elizabeth Taylor (again). She brings a murderer to justice (*The Painted Hills*) and saves an orphan from a fire (*The Sun Comes Up*).

By the time of her TV series, *The Adventures of Lassie*, Lassie had come to seem overqualified for her role, even for her species — too sensitive, too smart, too damn virtuous. I always had the feeling that the only reason she didn't just start talking French or playing the piano was that she didn't want to embarrass the rest of the family. In one episode, she gets hit by lightning and gets right up again. In another, Benji guest-starred as a city dog whom Lassie instructs in country ways. Remember the episode where she goes to law school and passes the bar in time to save the day at the Scopes trial? How about the one where she cracks a safe, solves a murder, and carries the diphtheria remedy to those poor people in Alaska? Oh, no, right, that was Balto.

Lassie's strangest accomplishment of all was in transcending time and breed to assume the role of a Skye terrier in Victorian Edinburgh. Remember the movie *Challenge to Lassie*? If you don't, I'm not surprised, since it's not really a standout, the combined presences of Donald Crisp and Edmund Gwenn (again and again) notwithstanding. The real significance of the movie is that it merges two annoying kinds of ideal dogs, the infuriatingly capable Lassie and the insufferably devoted Greyfriars Bobby, the Scottish Scamster.

I mean no disrespect to the Scottish, especially since my wife was born in Edinburgh, but to me the story of Greyfriars Bobby is the most sentimental, puerile, nauseatingly heartwarming dog story of them all. It has been told and retold in countless children's books, at least one adult novel, and two movies, a Disney version as well as the Lassie one, both featuring Donald Crisp. And both of them promulgate the same bilge, revealed as the tissue of lies that it is by none other than Forbes MacGregor, whose book *Greyfriars Bobby: The True Story at Last* blows the lid off a legend I have long viewed skeptically.

Greyfriars Bobby was, as you recall, a Skye terrier belonging to an Edinburgh policeman named John Grey. When Constable Grey died unexpectedly in 1858, his dog began a vigil at his master's grave that lasted fourteen years, until the dog's death. Today it is impossible to walk around Edinburgh without bumping into a Bobby statue or pub or souvenir store filled to overflowing with doodads celebrating the dog's loyalty.

There is a similar story in Japan that has grown up around a dog named Hachi-ko, an Akita, whose master didn't return home from work one day in 1925. The dog spent

277

the next nine years waiting at the train station. After his death, a bronze statue of the dog was erected there.

My critique of Greyfriars Bobby can be summed up this way: Hey, Bobby, get a life. There is a line between a suitable period of mourning and morbid preoccupation. You, Bobby, have crossed it.

Or so I thought, until I read MacGregor's book, where I learned that Bobby did not pass his days in mourning. He was a celebrity, ambling down to a local pub every day at the one o'clock gun along a route crammed with spectators. In bad weather, plenty of locals were happy to take him in. Without respite from the weather, it's doubtful he would have reached the ripe old age of sixteen. Age did not mellow him, apparently. Contemporary recollections recall a feisty creature who tried to pick a fight with every dog he met. Greyfriars Bobby parlayed the death of his master into a living.

Both film versions of the story dispense with Constable Grey, and, in both, Bobby is a dog from the countryside. In the Disney version, Bobby is a proper terrier, which makes no sense, since a terrier could never be a shepherd's dog. The shepherd would have a nervous breakdown. In *Challenge to Lassie*, the country connection is a feeble attempt to explain what a big rough collie is doing in Edinburgh. She seems out of place all over town except in the graveyard. Few can dream of a perpetual mourner as dignified as Lassie.

By the time Lassie came to television in 1954, she was no longer British. She lived on a farm in Calverton, U.S.A. Over the seventeen-year run of the series, Lassie was portrayed by eight different dogs. They were all bred and trained by Rudd Weatherwax, who, with various members of his family, also trained Asta in the *Thin Man* movies, Old Yeller in *Old Yeller*, and Toto in *The Wizard of Oz*. The first Lassie was male, and all subsequent Lassies have been laddies, too. Males are bigger, shed less, and look more imposing overall, especially when placed next to a child actor. (Toto, by the way, was played by a cairn bitch named Terry who appeared in ten other movies, working with the likes of Joan Crawford, Spencer Tracy, and Ida Lupino.)

Since Lassie's heyday, movie dogs have followed more or less the same trajectory as human actors. They are less heroic and imposing than the stars of old. Lady and the Tramp weren't heroic, but their affect was more Fred and Ginger than bitch and stud. Today's screen dogs are doggier. Sleek athletes like Lassie and Rinty have given way to lovable schlump Beethoven and Milo, the doughty pug of *Milo and Otis*. In *The Mask*, Jim Carrey's giant-hearted Jack Russell is neither too bright nor too well behaved. Neither is Frasier's. In *Down and Out in Beverly Hills*, the lovable family pooch is in therapy. The cowardice and insecurity of Santa's Little Helper, the Simpsons' dog, is essential to his appeal.

I know of only one dog movie that is not family fare. *White Dog*, based on a novel by Romain Gary, is about a stray, a ghostly white German shepherd adopted by the young woman who accidentally hit him with her car. Gradually the woman realizes that her new best friend has been conditioned to attack black people. She finds a trainer, a black man, who assumes the challenge of deprogramming a dog who's been programmed by racists. The movie is directed by Samuel Fuller, highly regarded for his noirish war and crime melodramas, many with terrific titles like *Shock Corridor*, *The Crimson Kimono*, and *The Naked Kiss*. *White Dog* is a little preachy about the ingrained nature of racism, but it's very well acted (by Kristy McNichol and Paul Winfield, among others), and the director creates a real atmosphere of dread around the dog, who is quiet and contained in all his scenes, except when he's mauling someone.

The film so disturbed its producers, Paramount, that they shelved it, saying it would encourage racist violence. Fuller left the country for the next thirteen years. The movie was well received in Europe, and Paramount finally released it as a TV movie in a version edited, apparently, to make it about a dog who attacked everyone, not just blacks. I can't imagine what they did to make the movie come out that way. Michael Eisner, one of the Paramount biggies who deep-sixed *White Dog*, brought further honor upon himself more recently as head of Disney, when the Mouse chickened out of distributing *Fahrenheit 9/11*. Copies of *White Dog* come on eBay once in a while. (Beware of tapes; mine was taken from a European television broadcast with German subtitles and a picture painful to watch. Hong Kong–made DVDs are much better.)

White Dog resonates because its story is built on a phenomenon that every dog person has observed: Dogs have biases just like human prejudices. They will discriminate against whole classes of people, not just individuals. They'll hate men in uniform or people in red. In white communities, sometimes it's black people they don't like. I was on the meadow one day when there was much levity about a new little dog on the scene who was running around and barking at people. Later I was strolling with a black friend and his giant schnauzer. My friend was annoyed. The little barky dog's owner had laughingly told him that her dog behaves that way only toward Hispanic and black men. "That's a little more information than I want," he said. "I'm out walking my dog. Handle your own issues on your own time."

I didn't tell him that George has barked at enough black people himself to make me concerned, or at least embarrassed on occasion. It has never become a regular thing, much less a predictable one. About three-quarters of the time George sees the giant schnauzer's owner, it's pats and wiggles and happy to see you. But the other quarter of the time, George barks at him in a way that would look much creepier if he were a bigger dog. So we work at it. George (and I) shall overcome.

MY DOG IN ART

I would rather see the portrait of a dog that I know, than all the allegorical paintings they can show me in the world.

— Samuel Johnson

The Highland Tod, painted in 1859 by Richard Ansdell, is a historic cornerstone of dog art. It depicts a foxhunter with his downed quarry slung across his back, passing amid some local people on a beautiful highland path. Deployed across the panoramic width of the canvas are a dozen dogs, precursors of most modern Scottish breeds. It's a beautiful scene, people and dogs traversing under a brilliant sky, snow-covered hills in the distance.

It pains me to say, then, that the painting has absolutely no credibility for terrier people. I mean, it's a nice picture and all, and it looks completely believable that the hounds and the setter would stick with their master in this setting, and the collie would stick close, too, but the terriers sure as hell wouldn't be toddling along behind the foxhunter. They'd be all over the place, probably right out of the frame of the picture, and then you wouldn't have those clear illustrations of the precursors of most modern Scottish breeds. The picture would have narrative integrity but it would be less impressive. It might even be better art, but it would be lesser dog art.

Dog art is not art that just happens to have a dog in it. A portrait of a Renaissance woman with an adoring toy pom by her side is not dog art. Dogs are in the thick of Rubens's *Wolf and Fox Hunt*, but that's not dog art, either, because even though the dogs are in the thick of it, the painting is not about them. The essence of dog art is that it's about dogs, first and foremost.

Perhaps for that reason, true dog art is a very small field, "a comma in the history of art," in the words of William Secord, who ought to know. He is the founding director of the AKC Museum of the Dog and the author of *Dog Painting* and *A Breed Apart*. Today his eponymous gallery is widely regarded as the finest repository of classical and contemporary dog painting in the world. He is more modest in his claims. "The very first-rate dog paintings, the best work of Stubbs and Landseer, those are all in museums or a few private collections," he says. "What's available is in that style, but it's not of that quality."

A dog painting does one of three things. It is a portrait of a loved one; it shows working dogs at work or sporting dogs sporting, doing what they're supposed to do; or it is a breed study.

Breed portraits came into being just about the same time that breed standards did. For this reason, Secord doesn't refer to dogs in pre–nineteenth-century paintings by specific breed names. He will refer to a mastiff-like dog or a spaniel-like dog, because it isn't technically correct to say more than that.

There are certainly a lot of beautiful dog paintings, but as a genre, dog art has issues. Or rather *I* have issues with it, issues concerning a certain narrowness of vision. First of all, while some dog art is of historical value (see above) and some is of artistic value (Stubbs, Landseer, George and Maud Earl), a whole lot of it is weak tea in the extreme, pretty pictures of pretty dogs without much effect. In 2000 a Manhattan art dealer named John Rosselli referred to all but the best dog paintings as "decorative art . . . people buy five or six and hang them on a wall."

As it happens, we have a couple of Victorian decorative paintings in our living room, but nothing so trivial as portraits of some dead rich person's dogs. No, one of ours depicts soldiers departing by ship for the Crimean War, and the second one shows them returning, much the worse for wear. They may not be great art, in fact I'm certain they're not, but they're certainly dramatic. Which is more than you can say for dog portraits.

Clearly, other people see things differently. There's usually a lavish dog auction or two in New York during the run-up to Westminster. In 2002, *Forbes* ran a piece about the surging popularity of commissioned pet portraits. The article covered some of the leading painters now at work and quoted an oil heiress saying "I'd rather sell my Rembrandt than my Beau Bradford." Commenting on the naked enthusiasm collectors have for this work, the *Forbes* writer felt compelled to point out that "while you have to be a pretty rabid pet-lover to commission such works, you don't necessarily have to be a philistine."

For those who are a little philistine, and I mean that in the nicest possible way, eBay is always full of dog paintings, tatty and less so, and for each of the eight artists *Forbes* highlights, there are dozens more advertising in magazines, on the Web and locally.

Most collectors of this stuff are breed-smitten, and often the more obscure the breed, the more desirable its image in art. Secord's previous dog was a Norfolk named Norah who is memorialized in a dreamily beautiful painting by Christine Herman Merrill. When I visited him, he had a Dandie Dinmont puppy named Rocky. Dandie Dinmonts are small, low-slung terriers with big, lambent eyes. The first time I saw a Dandie was at Westminster, and a woman next to me called it a Dandie Dickmutt. (Dandie Dinmont is a character from *Guy Mannering* by Sir Walter Scott.) Rocky is the only Dandie I've ever seen outside of a dog show, but there must be some around, because Mr. Secord says he can never keep Dandie Dinmont pictures in his gallery.

I guess it makes sense that dog lovers love dog art. But then I try to imagine a big oil painting of someone else's heroic-looking Victorian terrier over the mantel-piece, and I wonder why in the hell I would want that.

This brings me to the second problem I have with classical dog art, which is that it's unfair to George and all dogs built along less than majestic lines. Sure, a glorious Gordon setter coursing across a field of heather is a glorious sight, if indeed coursing is what setters do and heather is where they do it. And you can see where an artistic rendering of such a scene could make a lovely picture. Now picture a fine dachshund similarly in medias res: We see the little hound's ass disappearing down a badger sett.

I once saw a Norfolk breed study in the heroic mode. It was sitting in pride of place on an easel in the posh home of a breeder, with its own little track light focused on it. The picture showed a wild landscape, with rushing stream, lowering sky, dark forest, and, in front of it all, one paw resting on a downed tree, a Norfolk terrier, wearing an expression reminiscent of Douglas MacArthur's when he left Korea.

Nice picture, beautiful dog, but all I could think was: What's that little dog doing out there all alone, off-leash? Has he had his shots? Would he like a treat?

George is many things, but majestic is not one of them, although all witnesses were impressed the time in the park that he chased the beautiful gray great Dane, who was so surprised she took off, creating the impression that George had routed the enormous creature. George may have thought so, too, because he wheeled around in midcanter and went after the bigger black Dane who deftly smacked him aside with a front paw without so much as breaking stride.

George and his kind, I'm afraid, are made for caricature, not heroics. What, really, are George's heroic gestures? Climbing boldly into the dishwasher, the better to lick the plates? Rearing up on his stubby hind legs, as he barks urgently to warn us of falling dandelion spores? Growling ominously at the enormous golden retriever who rolls onto her back and pees whenever George walks by? (In that case, I think he growls out of embarrassment. I would.)

George's cartoonish qualities immediately appealed to me. That level of appreciation kicked in well before I was able to recognize his deeper qualities. There's a precedent here. Long before I cared about dogs, I spent a lot of time pondering some caricatures of them done by an artist named Constance Depler. If that name rings a bell with you, it's probably because you have spent time in cheesy bars like the one in which I spent the happiest hours of my university years.

The Royal Palms' decor was minimal, to put it mildly. Its chief decorative element was a mural that filled the entire wall across from the bar and catty-corner to the dark, dank dance floor. It was, I learned later, actually two murals placed side by side, *Hep Hounds* and *Bar Hounds*. In the former, a group of dogs dressed as people dance to a small canine combo. *Bar Hounds* shows similarly snazzy dogs sitting and standing at a bar, drinking. Closer inspection reveals that they are mostly the same dogs in two different settings, although some of them change outfits and genders. The natty Tony Randallish Boston terrier sitting at the bar is a jaded debutante with a bored expression on the dance floor. The barman (bardog?) of *Bar Hounds*, an Old English sheepdog who tips his head quizzically toward the morose basset hound (what other expression does a basset hound have?), is alone in the dance tableau, seated off to the side, having a little snooze. The basset, on the other hand, has changed from sport coat and straw skimmer to full flapper drag and is being steered around the dance floor like Margaret Dumont by what appears to be a Harpo-esque cairn terrier new in town.

The doofy great Dane in a sailor's middy blouse dances close with the same miniature poodle hottie he's chatting up at the bar. Less lucky barflies are the poor dachshund with no one to talk to and the braying, drunken Afghan, neither of whom makes it onto the dance floor. The Doberman with the Euro leisurewear seems to have bird-dogged the boxer in the cutaway. Not to worry, as the boxer seems to be making time on the dance floor with the overdressed cocker spaniel who seemed to be at the bar with Mr. Basset.

"Bar Hounds"

With their flat, dull backgrounds, the murals seem built more for durability and low maintenance than aesthetic pleasure, but pleasure trumps. They are full of detail and life, especially if you've been drinking, in which case their grandeur rivals that of *The Last Supper* or Monet's *Water Lilies*.

The breeds are rendered very distinctly, and the interaction and expressions of the dogs take on human complexity. The scenes invite speculation. I believe that, over the half century since they first appeared on the nation's barroom walls, countless hours of amiable, mostly nonviolent chat has been devoted to these murals, parsing the intricacies depicted, comparing the dogs to local people. Have a beer, look at the dogs, relax. The hound murals are more than caricatures. They are public art and agents of healing. Or at least they were at the Royal Palms, where, if you were sitting by the lower right-hand corner of their wall, you were just about at eye level with the name Constance Depler.

The name was well known to the students who frequented the place. Over the years I've seen the murals in some other bars; they have a long half-life. At a flea market, I found a tatty gray replica of the *Bar Hounds*. On eBay, I tracked down better versions of both, in the well-remembered Deck Paint Red. (Now, when Depleriana appears on eBay, I am routinely priced out.) But the Internet yielded nothing about Constance Depler: no fan sites, no academic monographs on her enduring legacy, no mentions in the advertising history newsgroup, nothing. I assumed Depler was an unsung wallpaper company employee who faded into oblivion.

So you can imagine my surprise when, in 2000, she called me.

At least the woman's voice on my answering machine said she was Constance Depler, calling from California. I kept her message for weeks, to replay when I disbelieved. Was it really her? The Palms murals were old and weathered in the 1960s, when I first saw them. How old was Constance now? How had she found me? How did she know I'd be interested in hearing from her?

Through Google, what else? I'd written a piece for my alumni magazine in which I mentioned the Depler murals fondly, and the piece was posted on the magazine's Web site. Constance found me by Googling her own name. She was coming to town for Westminster and suggested we meet at Keene's Chop House, which is not far from Madison Square Garden. Keene's is a venerable hunk of old New York, noted for its mutton chops and extensive malt whisky selection. If not literally a salad-free zone, it is not what you would consider a lady's restaurant. How promising that she suggested it for our meeting.

What can you say about a seventy-something-year-old legend who walks into the joint, offers a hug by way of hello, then leads the way to a table and orders double vodka rocks, followed by liver and onions medium rare? If you're me, you order exactly the same thing and tell her you've been a fan since you were old enough to drink. To say we hit it off is an understatement. Together we hatched plans for articles, books, possible world domination. But first I wanted to know where she'd been all my life.

Constance Depler is no two-mural wonder. She has had two entirely distinct artistic careers, which were separated, more or less, by the years she spent raising her children. Constance moved around a lot during her childhood, even touching down for a few years in Brooklyn in the 1930s, where her father was the first coach of the short-lived Brooklyn Football Dodgers (who knew?). After college, she settled in California. She and her husband, Pope, have been married for fifty-one years.

In the 1940s and 1950s, she was one of very few female artists working in advertising. It was the Golden Age of home entertaining, a sideboard heating tray in every home. Even my own mother, who had few ambitions as a hostess, had a fondue set and a coffee urn, though neither left their boxes much, or at all. All that gracious living meant an endless market for clever coasters, cocktail napkins, decks of playing cards, greeting cards, tea towels. Constance did a wonderful series of drawings based on famous paintings (*Mona Lisa*, *Blue Boy*, etc.), with dogs instead of people, that ended up on napkins. The *Bar Hounds* and *Hep Hounds* murals led to dogs playing baseball, in a barbershop, on the golf course. She drew tippling reindeer and poodles in the circus. Some of the wallpaper designs were sharp parodies of ads of the day. There's a chimpanzee who dreams she goes shopping in her Monkeyform Bra, and a colonial officer ape drinking gin. There are cocktail napkins with Old Master paintings on them and all the people replaced by dogs. (The sketchy paintings on the wall of the bar in *Bar Hounds* resemble these more finished parodies.)

Her work today is done under her married name, Constance Coleman, and in that guise she is one of the most distinguished pet portraitists in America. This isn't just my opinion; *Forbes* included her in that roundup of blue-chip pet painters.

Her clients include Oprah Winfrey and Oscar de la Renta.

Constance and Pope moved back to Cincinnati after twenty years in Carmel, California, to be nearer their grandchildren and the East Coast. After Westminster in 2004, she was off to Frisia to paint someone's Scotties for two weeks. Constance has an affinity for Scotties, or they for her. In 2003 the U.S. Scottish Terrier Club honored Constance for her work, I suppose in recognition of her recognition of how cute Scotties are. They do figure heavily in Constance's greeting cards, which are all done in her painterly portrait style.

It turns out that little pockets of Depler fans exist wherever the *Bar Hounds* hang. Two such cells thrive in Iowa, at the Dog House Lounge, which sells more beer than any bar in Dubuque, and at another venerable watering hole in Des Moines called The Greenwood. Given the devotion of Depler's fans, I once asked Constance why Caspari doesn't bring back the old stuff in a big way. They could rent display space at Westminster, sell the pieces at dog shows. She shook her head. "They don't want any anthropomorphic art," she said. "They feel it's making fun of what they do."

I was dumbfounded, especially having seen some of the junk that passes for respectable dog art. But it's true. Dog art has no room for camp, or whimsy. William Secord, the expert whose gallery has handled some of Constance's work, told me that most of Constance's current clients and admirers don't even know about her Depler days, and, if they do, they aren't terribly interested. They see it as a sort of Grub Street prelude to her more serious work, painting fancy dogs for fancy people.

Constance's paintings are warm and colorful, and look less formal to me than most official dog art. She calls them "life-style portraits," and they are in demand. But when I ponder the question of which artist could really do George justice (besides my son, whose sketches in pen on Post-it capture the essential George perfectly), it isn't Coleman I think of, or even Landseer or Stubbs. It's Depler.

MERCH

Over one hour of relaxing music laced with soft animal sounds to create a peaceful environment for pets who are left alone or when

the owner needs quiet time.
Created by a professional
composer experiencing problems
with his own pet who suffered
from separation anxiety . . .

— From liner notes for "While You Are
Gone," a CD of music for dogs

Deep in the recesses of a storage closet, on a
shelf that neither wife nor son can reach, is a
tightly wrapped package about the size of a
grapefruit. Inside layers of tape and bubble
wrap is a hand-blown glass object, about two
and a half inches by one and a half, that pur-
ports to be a representation of a Norfolk terrier. The figurine has a little hook behind the
head so it can be strung up on . . . what, exactly? A necklace? A Christmas tree? I really
have no idea and I can't really ask my wife
since I haven't had the nerve to show this
particular bauble to anyone.

I found the thing on eBay, where you
could get, and maybe still can, hand-blown
renderings of many different breeds, including obscure ones like the basenji.
Aside from coloring, they all look pretty
much the same. You can tell they're dogs
and generally if they're skinny or fat, but

the finer points aren't really there. The fact is that the medium of hand-blown glass is not well suited to the accurate representation of specific breed details. The thing isn't really pretty, nor is it ugly enough to be camp. At thirty dollars, it's not a bargain either.

Certainly this is a pretty low-flying example of having more money than taste, but it is also a demonstration of the fact that into every dog person's life, some tat must fall. And while there are all sorts of numbers available on what Americans spend on their pets, those numbers usually address things like food and vet bills. Most of the dog people I know do not want to know themselves, let alone reveal, how much they've spent on squeak toys or breed-specific drawer pulls or spaniel-size Halloween costumes.

As former caregiver to four red-eared slider turtles, I can assure you that the Dog World's flair for conspicuous consumption has no correlative in the herpetological world. For a splurge, you might get your turtle some feeder fish, ten for a buck, a sum that wouldn't buy an acceptable Yorkie-size chew toy.

Because I am an essentially non-materialistic, spiritual sort of person, I assume I'd be immune to the tchotchke tsunami that follows the acquisition of a pet. But sellers of pet merch target their market as accurately as AARP sniffs out new fifty-year-olds. I receive a constant barrage of e-mails and catalogs from Woof 'n' Meow, Meow 'n' Bark, Bark 'n' Purr, Purr 'n' Arf. After my initial spree, I restricted myself to a decorative brooch for my wife with a little decoupaged picture of a Norfolk from an old cigarette pack. My wife pronounced it "quite nice, really." I have passed on all Norfolk mouse pads and bumper stickers since then, but cuter stuff appears all the time. The next thing I knew, I was trolling the Web for it.

I didn't realize I'd crossed the line until the calendars arrived. That's calendars, plural. I was so sure the calender would be a hit I ordered two, recipient TBA. I gave one to my wife, no special occasion, just one of those wacky gestures that brings couples together. I'd gift-wrapped it, in my Neanderthalish way, to set up the surprise. She unwrapped it, and there it was: Monthly Doos, twelve months of arty photos of poo in seasonal settings — nestled in snow, by a waterfall, and so on. She was quite polite, but concerned as to whom I thought I might be giving the other calendar to. Later, when I returned them both to Mew 'n' Ruff, I looked for "spousal veto" among the reason for return options, but had to opt instead for my usual "didn't like styling."

Between pricey dog art and low-end dog kitsch, there is a vast range and a vast audience for it, even outside the fancy. I'm always surprised at how many dog people flaunt their breed affiliation in T-shirts and baseball caps. Devoted as I am to George and handsome as Norfolks are, I cannot for the life of me imagine wearing a picture of one on my shirt. Zillions disagree, and at dog shows, breed wear is a fetish. Fanciers embellish their English country drag with pins, medallions, sew-on patches, and stickpins. For men, there are club ties with dog heads. Many clubs use dog sculptures and figurines as prizes for their events.

Breed-specific paraphernalia always has a limited but ardent audience, and the best of it isn't cheap. Dog people know if the dogs don't look right. Omar Pitaluga makes his pendants, earrings, and other pieces in gold and silver. He has an advantage over most jewelers who do this kind of work. He is a dog person who does jewelry, not a jeweler new to the Dog World. How many other jewelers are also breeders of dogo Argentinos? To create his 200 molds depicting 160-odd breeds, Omar studies the winning dogs at the shows he visits regularly. He pores over *Dog Show* and the other magazines of the fancy. He talks to breeders. Who knew that a bulldog is supposed to be pear-shaped when viewed from above? Or that you're supposed to be able to see the back legs when looking through the front legs? "I deal with a public that's very picky," Omar says.

Omar's knowledge of so many different breeds didn't come overnight. His first attempt was a Doberman. When he showed it to the editor of the Doberman magazine that was going to advertise his numbered creations, she said, "This looks like Scooby-Doo," and began his education. Omar's bestsellers are cockers, Dobermans, great Danes: "Breeds that doctors and lawyers buy," he explains. He also does custom pieces that he'll base on specific dogs, if the client can provide a photo or two. But his great challenge is to represent all those breeds accurately and well. Even though, Omar says, he may not sell more than two or three pulik a year, he will continue to keep all the breeds available (and really, how many Filabrazilero pins can you sell?) because "if you can make a perfectly structured, accurate dog, you've got customers."

In William Secord's book, *Dog Painting*, I came across an oil of a couple of pugs smoking pipes by George Earl, one of the greatest Victorian dog artists and the father of another, Maud Earl. I was convinced I'd found the ur-Depler, the missing link between dog art and dogs playing poker. I was mistaken. Those dogs really were smoking pipes, Secord told me. It was a common Victorian parlor trick, as was training dogs to balance biscuits on their muzzles, then flip them up in the air and catch them.

I try to picture George doing either of these stunts. I don't think so.

Not that I care; George doesn't need props for his act.

8. from george to eternity

No matter how eloquently your dog barks, he cannot tell you that his parents were poor but honest.

— Bertrand Russell

Between 1935 and 1936 W. H. Auden and Christopher Isherwood collaborated on three plays. One of them, *The Dog Beneath the Skin*, was produced off-Broadway in 1947 with a cast that included future *Golden Girl* Bea Arthur. I have read *The Dog Beneath the Skin* three times. I believe it's either a political allegory very particular to the 1930s and thus hopelessly remote from me and my concerns, or an experiment in language very particular to the 1930s and thus hopelessly remote from me and my concerns. I can't make head or tail of the thing, actually, but I am pretty sure it's not about dogs. Still,

I choose to read and reread it for the same reason I often choose what I read, the belief that sometimes you *can* tell a book by its cover, and sometimes its title. I *love* that title. The dog beneath the skin is what every resident of the Dog World is after. I'm convinced there is a deeper understanding and experience of George's soul, mind, character, personality, whatever it is, if only I could find a way to get to it. Would the dog beneath George's skin resemble the George I know? I hope so.

There is pleasure in knowing that others before us, some of them great souls and minds, have wondered deeply about dogs. And when a smart person says something utterly inane about dogs, as plenty have, it's even better. Bemusement loves company.

There is no bemusement in Homer's description of Odysseus' return to Ithaca, recognized by no one but his faithful dog Argos, who, though blind and decrepit and without so much as a sniff or a pat from Odysseus in twenty years, manages to recognize his master just before dying:

Infested with ticks, half-dead from neglect,
here lay the hound, old Argos.
But the moment he sensed Odysseus
*   standing by*

he thumped his tail, nuzzling low, and
   his ears dropped,
though he had no strength to drag himself
   an inch
toward his master.

— Fagles's translation of *The Odyssey*

The sense of the awakened memory, the thump of the tail, the droop of the ears — you can just tell Homer was more than a poet, he was dog people, too.

I suspect ancient Greece was full of dog people. In his *History of Animals*, Aristotle notes that a Malossian-Laconian mix tends to be a healthier, more spirited creature than a purebred dog of either type, a clear recognition of the principle of hybrid vigor long before George Shull first documented it in maize plants in 1908. Aristotle may have been more than a dog person. His discussion of dogs' intelligence, temperament, and abilities is so detailed and knowledgeable that you feel he might have been an RB when he wasn't ratiocinating. The Greeks, by the way, knew about the antibiotic powers of dog saliva. I can't imagine how they figured that one out. Smelling it, you don't immediately think: *"Mmm, preventive!"*

Dogs in Europe would not have such compassionate and respectful masters for centuries to come. The rise of Christianity didn't help. The Good Book, it turns out, is full of bad dogs.

The mission of A Globe of Witnesses is "to reclaim the Anglican vocation of doing 'public theology.' " You may surmise correctly that theology is not my usual cup of chai, but I was drawn to an article on http://thewitness.org/ called "Treat Dogs as Dogs?" It described a growing chorus of Anglican voices saying that treating dogs with love and respect is against the teachings of the Bible, that being kind to animals is, in essence, un-Christian. The implications of this assertion are of course, far-reaching, especially if the scriptural interpretation at issue were to be taken up by other dominations. The Pope would have to rescind Francis of Assisi's sainthood. It would be a scandal.

I could hardly believe my luck at coming across such devout looniness, but then I noticed the dateline: 2010. I noticed that Cheney was prez, not veep, and I realized it was all a smart joke, but one with some truth to it. Dogs are not shown much TLC in either testament, and they usually don't deserve it either. They are viewed mostly as unclean pariahs:

> *As a dog returneth to his vomit,*
> *so a fool returneth to his folly.*

— Proverbs 26:11

That's a nice thing to say about our oldest domestic ally, is it? You can't really argue with the analogy, but surely there's a less dog-averse way to make the same point. If you're looking for insights into dogs, don't waste your time combing through the Bible. For your convenience, I've compiled every single positive reference to dogs in both testaments. Here they are, both of them:

In the Book of Tobit, the dog that accompanies Tobit's son Tobias on his quest is really the only benign, or at least neutral, portrayal of a dog in the entire Bible. The dog itself has no name; nevertheless, its mere presence has made Toby a popular name for dogs since the dawn of time, or at least before other human names came into common use. (In 2003, by the way, the most popular dog's name in New York City was Max.)

Then there are dogs who lick and soothe

Lazarus's sores. They're presumably kindly, but you still don't see many dogs named Lazarus around. You can't really blame people for not wanting to name a dog after an old beggar covered with sores who dies, even if he is resurrected.

Islam, with origins in the same part of the world as Christianity and Judaism, holds a similarly low view of dogs as unclean scavengers. Dogs aren't exempt from the new fundamentalism, either. In 2002 an Iranian cleric named Hojatolislam Hassani from the city of Urumiyeh denounced dog ownership as moral depravity and called for the arrest of all dogs and their owners. Specifically, his demand called for the "judiciary [to] arrest all dogs with long, medium or short legs — together with their long-legged owners. Otherwise, I'll do it myself." Another reason I won't be vacationing in Iran.

You'd assume that Buddhist countries would be more forgiving of their dogs. In China and Vietnam, though, dogs have long been eaten. In Thailand, dogs have rarely been on the menu; still, for many years Bangkok authorities euthanized them in large numbers. In 1998, a campaign undertaken by the Society for the Prevention of Cruelty to Animals argued that the practice violated Buddhist principles. Since then, the city has adopted a pro-life dog policy. Monks and other volunteers routinely round up dogs, feed them, treat medical problems, neuter those who aren't already fixed, and return them to the streets. In 2002 the king of Thailand, Bhumbibol Adulyadej, wrote *The Story of Tondaeng*, about the stray he'd adopted, to encourage more people to do the same. The book was popular but had little effect on adoptions. In 2004, according to the *Wall Street Journal*, planning began for a massive kennel in Bangkok that would house 8,000 dogs, a fraction of the dogs on the street. The mayor, a Buddhist, has said the dogs discourage tourism, and it is necessary to put aside religious beliefs to handle the problem. Meanwhile, Bangkok's strays have become unusually tame, even friendly.

Community dogs, supported by many but belonging to no individual, are found all over Asia (in Kathmandu, they represent about half the dog population, while individually owned pets account for only 5 percent) and Latin America, but rarely in Europe or North America (with the notable exception of Ithaca, New York). Why this lack of compassion for the species that we Americans were first to call man's best friend?

I blame René Descartes, the DWEM of DWEMs.

Despite the disparagements of scripture, the idea that animal intelligence was essentially similar to the human kind has dominated folklore, literature, and art. "The behaviour of animals . . . proceeds from a reasoning, that is not in itself different, nor founded on different principles, from that which appears in human nature," wrote David Hume in *A Treatise on Human Nature*.

The first significant dissenter from this generally agreed-on view was Descartes, the Dead White European Male who made the world safe for vivisection. Descartes asserted that dogs are simply elaborate machines; what we perceive in them as thought or feeling is simply involuntary response to stimulation, like the contraction of a pupil in bright light. If that's the case, no moral imperative prevents us from cutting dogs open to see what makes them tick.

Humans are different in that we have a soul, Descartes goes on, a divine element that gives us moral powers and choices. It allows us to be saved and go to heaven.

Soulless machines won't be making the trip, which means that there will be no dogs or cats in heaven, but also no cockroaches, rats, or termites. It also means that heaven is vegetarian, which could cause huge tie-ups at the Pearly Gates as saved souls by the millions ask to see the menu at the other place. So heaven is freed up for its deserving occupants and all those cunningly crafted but morally inert lesser beings are banished to outer darkness. This formulation provided the moral justification for centuries of animal experimentation and abuse. In *The Intelligence of Dogs*, Stanley Coren describes a disciple of Descartes, Nicolas de Malebranche, kicking a pregnant dog who'd stumbled into his way. The dog cries out and passersby remonstrate. Malebranche says, "Don't you know that it does not feel?"

It's hard to know how anyone who's ever spent any time at all with dogs could say they don't think or feel, even if their thoughts and feelings aren't quite the same as ours. And in fact, Descartes doesn't say that in so many words. He says bodies, any bodies, are machines, which is a much easier proposition to accept. Coaches and fitness instructors make similar statements all the time. According to a Descartes biographer, Richard Watson, Descartes makes only three references to dogs in his works. One is from *The Description of the Human Body*, and it begins: "If you cut off the end of the heart of a living dog, and through the incision put your finger . . ." and you can tell he's been there.

But the other statements are different in kind. In *The Passions of the Soul*, he equates canine learning with human learning, suggesting that if hunting dogs can learn not to fear the sound of guns, so can people. And he remarks to a colleague that "after you whip a dog six or eight times to the sound of a violin, the sound of the violin alone will make the dog whimper and tremble with fear." This happens to be the first recorded observation of a conditioned reflex, and in my view it also establishes Descartes as a miserable son of a bitch.

The two statements taken together seem to imply that dogs both think and feel, which leads to the presence of a soul, which leads to Catholic theology, which leads to . . . let's not go there. Descartes had a dog himself, some sort of Dutch farm dog named Monsieur Grat. Stories that he was very fond of the pooch seem dubious, since in 1648 he sent Monsieur Grat away to a breeder in France. For

Monsieur Grat, it was probably all for the best.

The idea that dogs are automata no longer carries much credence, but the Cartesian model persists in sneaky ways.

"There is no evidence that dogs have the kind of complex emotional lives and value systems that we do," wrote Jon Katz in an essay on *Slate*.

But if we accept that dogs don't have human emotions, does that assumption require that even the ones that look like human emotions are qualitatively different? When George sees the long-haired dachs Goldie, they sniff each other and canter in circles, heads bobbing toward each other in what I would think were air kisses if I didn't know better. Is that happiness or is that merely stimulation, some kind of animal excitement with no psychological component that we would recognize as happiness? Once you entertain that possibility, you start to wonder if your own sense of happiness is just a bunch of firing neurons. This is one of those discussion topics, like personal finance, that should never be raised after nine in the evening. So, in the words of my wife, "Of course George experiences happiness and there's no reason to look at that behavior and call it anything else."

Which leads me to wonder what George's greatest happiness is. Food would be right up there, as is playing with one of his toys when it's new or suddenly desirable for reasons beyond my reckoning (this is why we rotate George's plush and squeaky toys, moving them in and out of circulation).

My son believes that George's greatest pleasure is anticipation. "He's happiest when he's waiting by the door to go out for a walk," he says, and he's right. George stands there, chest held high and breathing fast, his legs poised so that he appears to be standing on tiptoe. His black nose grazes the astragal.

Nicholas Dodman, a behaviorist, writes in *The Dog Who Loved Too Much* about the shocked responses of colleagues when he treated dogs with psychotropic drugs such as Zoloft and Xanax. The idea that dogs could experience depression or anxiety broadens the emotional spectrum allotted to them. It means dogs have more than minds, they have psyches. As if their owners didn't know.

It's no secret that sometimes even very intelligent people can be obtuse, even without an ulterior motive like that Descartes. Take, for example, Ludwig

Wittgenstein. I admire Wittgenstein as much as the next guy and have for years. I mean, is there any doubt the man was very, very bright? But I think it's possible he may never have met a dog, judging by this passage from *Philosophical Investigations*.

A dog believes his master is at the door. But can he also believe his master will come the day after to-morrow? — And *what* can he not do here? — How do I do it? — How am I supposed to answer this?

Can only those hope who can talk? Only those who have mastered the use of a language. That is to say, the phenomena of hope are modes of this complicated form of life.

If Wittgenstein had met George, he'd know differently. There is only one possible reply to the suggestion that hope requires language: *Are you nuts?* Dogs live on hope. It fuels their every waking moment. Every time anyone in the house puts on shoes or gets up from the sofa, George hopes. When he hears the faint sound of a biscuit being broken in two, the hiss of a jar opening that could conceivably be a jar of peanut butter, he hopes. All methods of training dogs are built around the manipulation of hope. Maybe it's the way you train any sentient being. Hope springs eternal in the human breast, doesn't it? In the canine aorta, too.

Another Viennese intellectual was less measured in his doggish enthusiasm. Sigmund Freud was very devoted to his trio of chow chows, Jo-Fi, Lun Yo, and Lun. He was more than fond of them, actually. He used them with his analysands. Jo-Fi, his favorite, would lie close to some patients, and this would calm them. She also would rise and move about precisely when it was time to end the session, an interesting alternative to the clock that's always just over the patient's shoulder.

Ever since learning about Jo-Fi, I've imagined sitting in a shrink's office with a chow in the room. The shrink I visited in my teen years sometimes had a dog in his office, but it was a little thing and always asleep when I was there, which allayed my dog fears but made me feel my life was boring. Chows have thick coats and black tongues. They are not known for their playful miens. They are heavyset and take up space. You'd have to wonder what a dog that big is doing there. An enforcer, perhaps, making sure that people pay at time of treatment? What if the dog just sat staring at you like the shrink, two pairs of staring eyes for the price of one?

If Freud were a contemporary psychiatrist, he would have to pay supplemental insurance to bring his dog to work. Chows are considered aggressive breeds in many jurisdictions, and premiums reflect additional risk. I mean, what if the dog tried to join me on the couch? Sure, Freud said patients found that comforting, but I'll be the judge of that, thank you very much. Dr. Freud, you remember, smoked cigars until his jaw fell off, so his idea of relaxation may not be the same as our own.

Earlier I said that I belonged to no kennel or breed clubs, that I subscribed to no dog-related publications, and that my home was not overflowing with dog-related paraphernalia. The part about our decor is still true, aside from the *Bar Hounds* reproduction in the kitchen that was there long before George arrived. But I am no longer a dog person alone. I subscribe to *Bark* (subtitle: *dog is my co-pilot*). I belong to the Fellowship for the Interests of Dogs (FIDO), the American Norfolk Terrier Association, and the Yahoo Norfolk/Norwich Message Board. Pursuit of the dog beneath the skin has gotten under my skin, but sometimes it's hard to live up to George's needs.

George is very shaggy at the moment. Richard, his groomer, has injured his shoulder and is sidelined indefinitely, sending shudders through the Greater Metropolitan Norfolk and Norwich communities. Many cairn and border terrier people are going to be affected as well. Richard does hand-stripping, which is the proper way to groom terriers, because of their double-textured coats. To get out the loose strands of coarse outer coat without messing up the soft undercoat, you have to pull them out with your fingers. It is a painstaking skill that most RBs and professional handlers learn to do themselves, because hand-stripping groomers are as rare as Arabists in the CIA. When I visited Constance Coleman, we drove halfway across Cincinnati to drop off her Norfolk with a hand-stripper she'd found. I haven't found one in Brooklyn and so far, I'm up to the P's in the Yellow Pages (Posh Pets, Puppy Paradise, Purrfect Pets). Well, I did find one, but she said it would take five to six hours, which is more than George or I could stand. There's a hand-stripper in Philadelphia who comes up to New York every so often, but he doesn't do Brooklyn.

I'd have to borrow someone's living room and vacuum it carefully afterward.

It's not as if my wife and I haven't tried to learn how to hand-strip ourselves. We've asked and read and watched and practiced. We've both gotten pretty good at it, though most of what we get off ends up on our clothes or furniture rather than any of the receptacles we set up for the purpose. George yips and flinches the moment we touch him — quite unlike the dignified stoicism he displays toward Richard — and between the yipping and the flinching and our squeamishness, we're somewhat slower than the pros. Still, if we could just get George to sit still for three years, we'd do a great job.

George was almost as shaggy last August, when all of us went to the Norfolk Association's Summer Fun Day in Connecticut. I was looking forward to seeing him on the agility equipment (a small obstacle course with little fences to jump over, a teeter-totter to navigate, an A-frame to climb) and in the earth-dog demonstration. All the usual suspects were there from previous Norfolk gatherings and I was sure they'd appreciate George's many sterling qualities.

It didn't happen that way. George was

bigger and hairier than any of the other dogs, and Judith Felton told me politely she wouldn't mind seeing him drop a pound or two. George wasn't making too many friends on his own either. In the multicultural crush of Prospect Park, he is a bon vivant, but in North Stonington, surrounded by his own kind, he was withdrawn and edgy. We were first up for the earth-dog demo. I led him over to the instructor, who showed him a cage with two rats in it. He looked, pressed his nose to the wire, sniffed. I encouraged him heartily, as commanded by the instructor, but George had made up his mind. He raised his head, turned around, and walked away with his tail down. I led him back a few times, but he just wasn't interested.

Someone asked, a shade mockingly, "Is he scared?" I recalled the pit mix George encountered on the Long Meadow the week before. They sniffed each other and then the mix did something that offended George. He turned on that dog with such sound and fury, though no actual contact, that the poor pit ran off, revealing that, in addition to being twice George's size, he was also intact.

"I don't think so," I replied stiffly. As we moved on and the next terrier approached the cage, I heard a voice I recalled from the first Norfolk event I attended. It was screaming, "Get rat-get-rat-GET-RAT!"

After lunch, a little racetrack was set up, with a starting box like the ones used for greyhounds but sized for Norfolks. A bit of fur served as a lure. George was the first in the little box and three other dogs went in with him. The fur was waved across the front of the closed box, presumably to give the dogs a sniff that would incite their nascent bloodlust, and then it was attached to a makeshift pulley. The front side of the starting box fell open, the lure started to move, and three dogs tumbled out of the box after it, followed by George, who ran right off the course looking for us. He was vexed; people laughed.

Someone had set up a kid's wading pool and put a few inches of water in it for the dogs. George led us over to it and sat. Other dogs joined him. He paid no attention to them or us; he just sat and smoothed his coat. After a few minutes, he stood up, led us over to the agility area, and went through the entire course without a pause. We left a little while later, feeling obscurely miffed. On our way back to Brooklyn, my son said, "They made me feel like we're all hippies, including

George." George got a lot of treats that night.

Friends called recently. One of them was about to have a baby and had gone into the earliest stages of labor. They were making plans for their Australian shepherd, Jackson. He doesn't like to be alone, especially since his longtime companion, a sweet old rottweiler named Carly, had died a few weeks earlier. So they asked if we could take Jackson for the night.

It seemed completely doable, a treat. Jackson is not a stranger in our home. During the big blackout of 2003, we'd had both our friends and Jackson and Carly over because our fridge was full. I made scrambled eggs and spinach for all of us, and we hurried to drink as much white wine as possible before it got too warm. Candles shed a little light, and all around the table in the outer darkness we heard the big dogs pacing and panting, moving in close from time to time for a gentle lean or just to breathe on a knee, which is impossible for George. It was divine.

But this time Jackson would be without Carly and without his people, and there'd be no way to explain it was only temporary. And what would George make of it? He and Jackson are mutually well disposed, they've even spent some afternoons at Eva's, where Jackson is a newbie, but they're not what you would call intimates.

Our friend showed up with Jackson and his overnight bag of essentials: water, kibble and bowl, well-worn pillow. George wanted it all, loitering enthusiastically underneath the dining room table where we'd put the bag, trying to figure out how to get up there without our noticing. At least that's what I think he was plotting. He looked kind of desperate, laying siege even when we put the thing out of reach.

George barked initially, in a way that seemed to combine greeting and warning. The dogs sniffed each other, tails beating metronomically. George jumped up exuberantly to lick Jackson's nose; Jackson took it in stride. But when his owner left, the tone shifted a little. My son, eager to be a good host, petted and talked to Jackson. Jackson's response showed our boy, for the first time, that not all dogs are as impervious to the blandishments of petting and attention as George. Some dogs luxuriate. And as the two of them stood there leaning into their lovefest, here came George, dashing the length of the living room, barking with intent and interposing himself between boy and dog like a chaperone at a prom breaking up the close dancers. It was the most naked demonstration of possessive jealousy I've ever seen George express. Mellow Jackson immediately backed off and the two dogs sniffed some more, wagged in a well-intentioned if desultory way, and then moved to opposite sides of the house. Jackson stood by the door, then sat by the door, occasionally uttering a sighing whimper.

The evening passed quietly. Jackson drank out of George's very small water bowl and George drank from Jackson's much larger bowl. We retreated to our bedroom for the air-conditioning. Jackson amiably lolled on our son, while George patrolled in circumspect fashion, occasionally coming in to sniff his boy, then moving away to keep his own counsel under the wing chair by the window. The big dog lay athwart the boy, who was massaging the dog's head and chin. When he slowed, Jackson batted him gently with his front paw, demanding more. Eventually Jackson tired him out and he loped off to bed. The four of us, man and wife and two dogs, settled for the night.

George usually sleeps in a cramped space between my nightstand and the wall. There's a little mound of well-kneaded towels there that he occasionally feels the need to rearrange vigorously and without warning at odd hours of the night, disconnecting the phone jack as he wedges himself just so. Jackson, exploring the room, wandered over to the little space and sniffed the towel. In the corner of my eye, I saw George lurking under the chair, watching Jackson keenly. I didn't want Jackson to sleep on my side of the bed, because then how would I get out? I gave him a big hug and gently dislodged him from George's corner. Jackson lay down flush with the end of our bed. George came over to his usual spot and sniffed but didn't stay. He returned to his fortress of solitude under the chair. And so we all slept. I always get up once or twice during the night, and every time I did Jackson stood, as if he'd been lying there waiting for me to arise. He would look deep into my eyes, as if asking "Do you need me, sire?" I don't mind telling you, it made me nervous.

The next day I was very proud of George, even if he did persist in trying to steal Jackson's kibble. He'd been a gracious host, sharing space, water, and other pack comforts with an outsider. And when the outsider began to get too close to my son for George's comfort, George broke it up once, to make his views known, then re-treated under the chair, like Achilles brooding in his tent. In the morning he could afford to be magnanimous. And when Eva's van came by to pick them up, they went like happy campers. Even though Australian shepherds are consid-ered one of the most intelligent of all breeds, and Norfolk terriers are mere problem-solvers, I had the distinct feeling that Jackson had been played by George.

One of the striking qualities of canine in-telligence, aside from the difficulty of de-fining and measuring it, is how unimportant it is to the human-dog relationship. Con-sider Rico, the border collie who under-stands 200 words and can assemble sentences. He is certainly an impressive creature (though not, in my view, as im-pressive as the 104-year-old parrot dis-covered last year in a British plant nursery who declaims "Fuck the Nazis" with im-peccable Churchillian diction). Very nice, but would you want Rico for a pet? I pro-pose a *Lassie* remake called *Rico, Come Home*. In this version, Rico sneaks off to the kennel-keeper's laptop, books the cheapest flight to Edinburgh, and finds Roddy MacDowell's place with the help of an improvised GPS device rigged from liver treats and the tinfoil packet they come in. With intelligence like Rico's, the homing instinct is really passé. Border collies are the MacArthur Fellows of dogs. They're also the decathletes of dogs, the Einsteins of dogs, the Picassos, Aretha Franklins, Reinhold Niebuhrs, and Derek Jeters of dogs. No wonder they make me nervous.

"It's a terrible thing to be a dog and to know you're a dog," says one of the articulate, accomplished, and doomed protagonists of *Lives of the Monster Dogs* by Kirsten Bakis. In this wonderful, unique book, the dogs of the title have been bred for intelligence as well as strength and power and then mechanically altered, fitted with voice boxes and articulating hands. The result is an ineradicable sense of shame at their animal nature.

Fortunately, that is not yet a problem real dogs have to face. I have seen George deeply embarrassed but never ashamed. The reflective capacity needed to feel shame isn't in him. George is what he is, an existential fact. So what if he doesn't drape himself all over you at the first sign of attention? This is a dog prepared to fling himself at the windowpane to protect this home from invaders. If he doesn't have the time to lie down every time somebody pets him, cut him some slack. Did he ask me to run eight blocks carrying him in my arms because he hurt his foot? No. Did he ask me to postpone my birthday dinner out with family just because he threw up as we were leaving? He did not. I voluntarily postponed it, knowing full well that "postpone," in my world, means "fuggedaboutit." I knew that George needs nothing so much as the presence of us, his pack, somewhere in the immediate vicinity. I knew also that leaving George home alone while I had doubts about his well-being, even ridiculously minor doubts, would mean an evening spent on tenterhooks, whatever they are. It's not worth it.

I love that he is such a modest little dude. We've just had Jackson for a second night, in the course of which he developed a violent stomach upset. I managed to sleep through most of it, while my wife sat dazedly in the yard in her PJs in the humid dark, while poor Jackson attended to his business. He got extra petting and concern in the morning, of course. George sensed it. But instead of getting, well, all *pissy*, he trotted around in a cheerful, public-spirited sort of way, battling his squeak toy to the ground, licking our sleepy son's entire head, periodically checking in on Jackson's bowl. He was in master-of-ceremonies mode.

I still like the idea of doing more with him — clicker training, the fox-trot, whatever. Truth is, however, I'm content, more than content, with George as he is, though I wish he'd cool it toward the long-suffering UPS man. I know there are what trainers call "teachable moments" all through the day, but I don't see either of us exploiting them much. I'd rather take George for a walk. He'd like that. No need to search for a plastic bag, they're sticking out of the pockets of every garment I own. I'm tired, I'm busy, the weather is awful.

He's staring at me.

appendix:
some favorite dog books

Before George, the last canine-centric book I read was *Old Yeller*, back in something like seventh grade. I have been making up for lost time. The literature is vast. Here are some of my favorites:

Stanley Coren has written extensively on canine intelligence and history. I recommend *The Intelligence of Dogs*, *The Pawprints of History*, and *How to Speak Dog*.

No one writes more eloquently about the politics and consequences of breeding practices than Mark Derr in *Dog's Best Friend*.

My Dog Tulip by J. R. Ackerley is a portrait of a marriage between an eccentric British bachelor and the German shepherd who loves him. The book's comedy, of which there is a lot, comes from the contrast between Ackerley's refined sensibility and Tulip's unreconstructed dogginess. The writing is droll and delicate. "Tulip's intestines have a debit as well as a credit side, and while the latter is sometimes a vexation to others, the former can be a serious inconvenience to me." Ackerley never goes sentimental or condescending. He treats Tulip as a true friend and partner and tries keenly to understand her on her own terms. "Tulip never let me down. She is nothing if not consistent. She knows where to draw the line, and it is always in the same place, a circle around us both. Indeed, she is a good girl, but — and this is the point — she would not care for it to be generally known."

Elizabeth Marshall Thomas takes her dogs seriously, too, so much so that they seem more human, more enlightened, in every way superior to the people in *The Hidden Life of Dogs*.

Lost and Found, Elizabeth Hess's memoir of working at an animal shelter in upstate New York, is more about the people than the animals, and manages to be a terrific read, despite the awful grimness of the subject.

Pack of Two, Caroline Knapp's meditation on dogs and people, is full of compassion and wit.

My favorite breed dictionary is Desmond Morris's *Dogs*. By far the most modestly produced of big-breed books, this one has simple line drawings instead of color pictures and the most breeds by a wide margin.

I've perused many training guides, and I find them all, even the ones that make sense, slightly annoying. Perhaps of necessity, they rest on the tacit assumption that the trainer knows what's going on inside a dog's mind, which strikes me as a vanity hardly justified by the ability to get a dog to sit and stay. Still, they are useful and necessary. My favorite is *Good Owners, Great Dogs* by Brian Kilcommons and Sarah Wilson. It breaks down training tasks into approachable units with lots of photos of Kilcommons bewitching assorted dogs into doing what he wants. The approach is friendly and reward-based, the writing is chatty.

Fiction about dogs usually involves attempts to divine the canine mind. In shimmering prose, *Flush* answers the question: What would it be like if a dog were as sensitive and self-aware as Virginia Woolf? Jack London tried to channel the dog mind in *White Fang* and *The Call of the Wild*, and his dogs turned out to be Hemingwayesque.

Kirsten Bakis's *Lives of the Monster Dogs* is about highly evolved, mechanically advanced dogs living in New York City on the Lower East Side. It's mysterious, moving, and smart.

William Secord's *Dog Painting* is a sumptuous coffee table book that is also a considered history.

Harriet Ritvo's *The Animal Estate* takes a broad view of the role of animals in Victorian England.

acknowledgments

A great many people have generously shared their time and expertise with me in preparing this book. Any mistakes are my bad, not theirs.

Heartfelt thanks to Barbara Miller, Kay McKinstry, E. Pope and Constance Depler Coleman, Fran Wright, Steve Esposito, Judith Felton, Robert and Henrietta Lachman, Jamie Wolf, Judy Gingold, David Freeman, Tyril Frith, Maurice Grabbett, Norman Parker, D.V.M., Omar Pitaluga, Ruth Remington, Sam Edwards, Lucky, Sam Greenhoe, Melisa Coburn, Chris Gillespie, Laura Laterman, Betsy Carter, Ann Powell, Susan M. Ely, William Secord, Tracy Rudsitas, John and Liddy Baker, Nat LaMar, Bonnie Dalzell, Dr. Robert L. Seitz, Susan and Jerome Vitucci, Martha Hirst, April Scott, Richard L. Reynolds, Brian Kilcommons, Deborah Manheim, Edward I. Koch, Henry Stern,

Elizabeth Hess, James Gleick, Cynthia Crossen, Gregg Miller, Mark Derr, John Buskin, Eva, Riley, Beate, Gosha, Anya, Christine and Adrian of Eva's Play Pups, Rachel McPherson of the Good Dog Foundation, Andrew N. Rowan of the Humane Society, Dr. Steve Zawistowski of the ASPCA, Barbara Colt of the American Kennel Club, Tupper Thomas, Mary Fox, Amy Peck and David Rainey of the Prospect Park Conservancy, and Vera Filipelli of Derby Lane Greyhound Track.

Thanks as well to Gerry Howard and Jennifer Carlson for their wise counsel and to Bronwyn Prohaska for her help with the research.

Thanks to my wife, Helen Rogan, and my son, Toby, for more than I can say.

If only George had more sense of occasion, I know he would want to administer a warm sniff of the anal glands to his many friends, including but not limited to Amy, Arrow, Astro, Bailey, Boris, Cassie, Daisy, Elliot, Francis, Lucky, Jean-Claude, Cody, Ajax, Patches, Otis, Jackson, Jackson, Jackson, Dolly, Phoebe, Nina, Paul, Terry, Frida Kahlo, Melvin, Charlie, Terry, Gunther, Ruby, Ruby, Lola, Lucy, Lucy, Lucy, Zimi, Tobias, Kermit, Shaka, Buster, Sweetie, Rock, Rocky I and Rocky II,

Watson, Watson, Wilson, Higgins, Higgins, Shakespeare, Marlowe, Webster, Turbo, Radio, Stereo, Moxie, Macy, Maggie, Chester, Stella, Stanley, Stella, Blanche, Gus, Blackie, Michael, Jenny, Miles, Joe, Ursula, Alice, Boris, Snowflake, Truffle, Sebastian, Sebastian and Red, Nigel, Austin, George the other Norfolk, George the great Dane, George the great Dane mix, all dogs named George everywhere, Audrey, Missy, Square Bear, Big Bear, Bear, Rocky, Maxie, Mona, Sophia, Jazz, Enid, Edith, and Goldie.

about the author

Alfred Gingold's books include *Snafu University* and the bestseller *Items from Our Catalog*, a parody of the L.L.Bean catalog. His articles on dog-related matters have been featured on *Slate* and in the *New York Times*. Gingold lives in Brooklyn with his family and, of course, their dog, George.

The employees of Thorndike Press hope you have enjoyed this Large Print book. All our Thorndike and Wheeler Large Print titles are designed for easy reading, and all our books are made to last. Other Thorndike Press Large Print books are available at your library, through selected bookstores, or directly from us.

For information about titles, please call:

(800) 223-1244

or visit our Web site at:

www.gale.com/thorndike
www.gale.com/wheeler

To share your comments, please write:

Publisher
Thorndike Press
295 Kennedy Memorial Drive
Waterville, ME   04901